365 DAYS

of

DIVINE
FEMININE
WISDOM

365 DAYS

of

DIVINE
FEMININE
WISDOM

DAILY GUIDANCE *for* *the* GODDESS WITHIN

MORGAN MIGLIORISI

HAY HOUSE

Carlsbad, California • New York City
London • Sydney • New Delhi

Published in the United Kingdom by:
Hay House UK Ltd, The Sixth Floor, Watson House,
54 Baker Street, London W1U 7BU
Tel: +44 (0)20 3927 7290; Fax: +44 (0)20 3927 7291; www.hayhouse.co.uk

Published in the United States of America by:
Hay House Inc., PO Box 5100, Carlsbad, CA 92018-5100
Tel: (1) 760 431 7695 or (800) 654 5126
Fax: (1) 760 431 6948 or (800) 650 5115; www.hayhouse.com

Published in Australia by:
Hay House Australia Ltd, 18/36 Ralph St, Alexandria NSW 2015
Tel: (61) 2 9669 4299; Fax: (61) 2 9669 4144; www.hayhouse.com.au

Published in India by:
Hay House Publishers India, Muskaan Complex, Plot No.3, B-2,
Vasant Kunj, New Delhi 110 070
Tel: (91) 11 4176 1620; Fax: (91) 11 4176 1630; www.hayhouse.co.in

A catalogue record for this book is available from the British Library.

Tradepaper ISBN: 978-1-78817-845-7
E-book ISBN: 978-1-4019-7004-8
Audiobook ISBN: 978-1-4019-7005-5

Printed and bound in Great Britain by Clays Ltd, Elcograf S.p.A.

To my parents.

Thank you for always

believing in me.

CONTENTS

INTRODUCTION

"Without us, Wild Woman dies.
Without Wild Woman, we die. Para Vida,
for true life, both must live."

— Clarissa Pinkola Estés, Ph.D.,
Women Who Run With the Wolves

They say there is a woman behind all great things birthed into the world. Just as women everywhere have continuously held important roles throughout the unfolding of history, you too have an especially important role to fulfill in your lifetime.

In ancient days, women were revered for their intuitive, healing, and leadership qualities. If you look to ancient Egyptian artwork, you see women being depicted as having authority over men. Likewise, there are many powerful goddesses from various belief systems all around the globe who were worshipped as leaders, teachers, and Divine Mothers.

When ancient civilizations fell, the wise old ways of women fell with them. The grand pendulum swung, and humanity shifted from a matriarchal society to a patriarchal one. Authenticity and individuality within every being were tossed to the side as the patriarchy called for structured order. With the new patriarchy, a rigid machine was imposed on societies around the globe, in which all humans and nature became merely cogs.

When masculine energy began dominating over feminine, the attitude toward women changed, like day to night. Women transitioned from being powerful authority figures, wisdom-keepers, and priestesses to being ridiculed, persecuted, and even murdered for embodying their true magical selves. In this new way of being, women's intuition, natural healing modalities, and living in unity with Mother Nature were replaced by logic, modern medicine, and ignorance regarding our cyclic nature. No longer were we recognized for our divinity and our interconnectedness with all living things; our ancient practices became something to laugh about. The goal of man was to conquer, control, and force. Under patriarchal reign, humanity lost the sacred feminine values of peace, unity, and love. This is where humans have remained for the last few thousand years.

By no means am I saying that men, logic, modern medicine, or even the way our daily life has evolved, are bad things. I am saying that due to the imbalance created between these two energies, collectively we have become unhealthy in mind, body, and spirit. Over the last few centuries, we have seen an increase in pain, hatred, and destruction. Humanity is completely divided, with society and media ensuring things stay that way. Due to patriarchal conditioning, humans have learned to live in their toxic masculine energy and have suppressed their feminine energy altogether.

We fight against each other, always needing to be right or to be on top. Our mentality has shifted from abundance for all, to all for one. We are rarely grounded in our present moments, always rushing through our journeys to reach the elusive *destination.* We have shown little respect for our home and are depleting our planet of its resources and wildlife. We are always on the go, never stopping to communicate with ourselves or nature. As a result, we have become disconnected from each other, but more importantly, we have become disconnected from our true Source.

The time has come for the pendulum to swing again. Enter Divine Feminine energy.

Now that Earth and humanity have had an extended dose of operating primarily in feminine energy (in ancient days), and then in masculine energy (the last few thousand years), it is time for the two energies to find balance and harmony with each other. If humanity is to thrive as it did in ancient days, and if Earth is to be restored, balance between these two energies must be attained. Just as feminine energy led previously, feminine energy will pave the way for this New Era to be birthed as well. This is where women take charge.

If you are reading this book, your soul has chosen an extremely exciting time to be on Earth. We are rewriting the way things have been for many centuries as we evolve together. Divine Feminine energy is reawakening, re-wilding, and reclaiming her lost power.

Unleashing our inner feminine energy is the key to creating balance on our planet. Every person, no matter their gender, contains both feminine and masculine energy within. The Divine Feminine within us all is being called to lead this global energetic revolution. The time has come for us to remember who we truly are at our core. Each of us is a goddess embodied. Each of us has mystical and intuitive abilities lying dormant within. This is the essence of the omnipresent Divine Feminine, and she has waited a very long time to be revived.

As we awaken to our truth and allow the ancient wisdom within us to come through once more, we become empowered. As we become empowered, we choose to trust our intuition, listen to our inner guidance, and move in flow with All That Is. Our lives become completely our own as we fearlessly speak our truth, exuding strength and grace as we choose to love ourselves and move to the beat of our own drum. Our energy changes, our vibration rises, and we move into higher love and enlightenment.

Everyone we come across will feel the touch of the Divine Feminine in our auras and witness her in our actions. The energy of the Goddess is so potent that as one person chooses to align with her, that choice sparks the beginning of the same journey within others. As more and more people embrace their inner wild woman and inspire others to do the same, a ripple effect emerges. This wave of high vibrational energy spreads throughout the world, igniting, awakening, and empowering the masses. It is our role as Divine Feminines to recognize our innate power and wisdom, activate it within ourselves, and share our unique gifts with the world. Through our examples of powerful feminine love, the world changes and a better tomorrow is created for all.

You are needed on this planet now, more than ever before. You have within you an incredible power. Your inner goddess is waiting for you to call on her and embrace that power. Your awakening is exactly what humanity and Earth need, not only to thrive but to *survive*. Together, we are breaking free from our cocoons, spreading our wings, and rising as Divine Mothers, birthing a New Age in the Old Ways.

ANSWER HER CALL

When you first remember that you contain within you the literal power to create worlds, you may feel intimidated. Your shadow side may creep in and tell you that you are not worthy of such a power. This stems from the many years of patriarchal conditioning and suppression your feminine energy has endured, in this lifetime and in lifetimes past. You may doubt yourself and your abilities, but there is something you need to know: you are a goddess, and it is your divine birthright to utilize your innate power. You were chosen to do this work and you are needed.

People everywhere are working together to bring back the ancient ways of the feminine, ushering in a period of Heaven on Earth. This New Era goes by many names: the Age of Aquarius, Ascension to the Fifth Dimension, New Earth, and more. No matter its name, the most important thing is its *vibration*. The foundation of this new beginning and universal shift in frequency is *love*. We are entering a time when humanity will live and thrive in love.

Collectively, we are releasing all that no longer serves humanity, and we are saying good-bye to the toxic ways of the patriarchy. We are closing the gaps where people are divided and creating harmony among all living things. We are remembering the truth of who we are and rebuilding our connection with Source.

The birth of a child is not an easy task—anyone will tell you that. And if it takes a village to raise a child, can you imagine how many it will take to raise a brand new world? Being tasked with birthing a New Age is not easy. There will be many times on your journey when you will feel like quitting, running away, and "going back to sleep." Awakening your inner goddess is one of the most intense experiences you will ever have in your lifetime. There will be many low points as you purge all aspects of you and your life that no longer serve you. There will be plenty of times when you feel the Divine Mother pushing you out of your comfort zone. But just as with any birth, your rebirth is sacred and will be absolutely beautiful. You will not regret a single moment of this journey.

If at any time you feel overwhelmed, unworthy, or all alone, call on the Divine Feminine, the Goddess. She will show you that you are resilient, you are powerful, and you are very far from alone. The Goddess will always be happy to cradle you and support you as you move forward to do her work. And in our 3D reality, there are many women all over the world who are awakening to their true nature. If you ask the Goddess to unite you with your soul sisters, she will.

The Divine Feminine energy that surges through my vessel is the same that surges through yours. No one is more important than another, and every single one of us is needed. We are the incarnated Divine Feminine collective, and we are here with a purpose: to spread love and light wherever we go, assisting the ascended Divine Feminine with birthing a new reality for all Earth's children to enjoy.

I am not saying anything here that you don't already know. There is a fire rising in your belly, and it is guiding you down the path of awakening. Your inner goddess is ready to emerge. She knows Earth is changing, and she is eager to be a part of this energetic reset. She is delivering you to your divine destiny.

Answer her call by going within yourself. Awaken your Divine Feminine energy by tuning in to the ancient knowledge held deep within your soul. As you embrace her, your life changes. With the recognition of your power comes strength. With the sharing of your wisdom comes courage. And with belief in yourself comes the ability to speak and *live* your ultimate truth. Through the embodiment of these virtues, your inner goddess blossoms. As you show her to the world, you learn the ultimate value: self-love.

It is your love for yourself that creates the wave of awakening that will take place all around the world. When you love yourself unconditionally, you are not afraid to be who you really are. You wake up every morning knowing your worth, while crafting a life that is genuinely yours. Your fearless authenticity is what inspires others to rise too. When more and more people, no matter their gender, get a taste of this pure Divine Feminine energy and all that she stands for, they will be eager to embody their true divine nature as well. As this takes place, the world changes.

Do you see how we are all working together here? And do you see why your light is so valuable? You were born to be a part of this universal movement. You are here to be a leader of this change. Have faith and believe in yourself. You are ready to remember the truth of who you are. You are ready to allow your inner goddess to emerge. No matter what your journey looks like, or how you share your wisdom, you are doing your part. Your commitment and devotion to yourself are all that is truly asked of you.

This is the path of the Divine Feminine. When one goddess heals, all heal. When one goddess emerges, all goddesses emerge. Slowly and steadily, feminine energy is restored all over the planet, expanding throughout the cosmos and changing the course of our history—*herstory*—forever.

For the sake of all living beings, answer her call.

HOW TO USE
THIS BOOK

The best way to incorporate Divine Feminine wisdom into your life and awaken your inner goddess is to work with her teachings daily. Before I began my own daily practice, I used to sway in and out of a spiritually based life. I was extremely dedicated to exploring my intuition, practicing divination, and reading as many spiritual books as I could find; then I wouldn't touch any of my card decks or books for months. I'd circle around and be really into it for a while, just to fall off it again.

But when I realized my inner goddess was demanding devotion and began to work with Divine Feminine wisdom daily, my life changed. My intuition became much stronger, and I felt more confident when acting on the guidance I received. I developed a stronger relationship with myself and learned how to love myself unconditionally. I recognized the importance of self-care, slowing down, and going with the flow. I found my voice and my inner power.

It is my intention to help you welcome Divine Feminine energy into your daily life so that you may do the same, and blossom in your unique way. This book is intended to spark a remembrance of the wisdom you hold within, and to help you *live* by that wisdom on the daily.

UNDERSTANDING FEMININE AND MASCULINE ENERGY

To understand the full scope of the energy that resides within you, it is vital that you know the gifts both feminine and masculine energy provide you.

When in balance, feminine energy is intuitive, loving, creative, and trusting. It is this energy within people that helps them be vulnerable, connect with others, and tune in to their nurturing abilities (whether it be toward the self or another). This energy is where a person's intuition and inner guidance comes from. When imbalanced, feminine energy can be inauthentic, manipulative, and codependent.

When balanced, masculine energy is action oriented, protective, logical, and accountable. It is this energy within people that helps them act toward their goals, provide stability for themselves and their loved ones, and protect who or what is most important to them. When imbalanced, masculine energy becomes controlling, competitive, withdrawn, and aggressive.

A woman may carry more feminine energy, but because she has both energies within her, she can tap into her masculine energy when she needs to. The same goes for men. Feminine and masculine energy are equally important, and we need to develop both inner energies to become truly whole beings. In essence, for us to be at our best, both energies need to be in harmony with each other. The problem we are facing as a collective is that we have neglected our inner feminine energy, resulting in the dominant masculine energy becoming toxic. If you look at both energies, examining their properties, you can see how the reign of the imbalanced masculine has had a negative impact on our world. Likewise, you can see why it is so important that we all allow our inner feminine to rise.

It will take time for you to feel comfortable embodying each balanced trait of the divine energies. Awakening and claiming your feminine power is a lifelong journey. There will be days when you are better at it, and days when you feel you need improvement.

During these times, remember that you truly are a Divine Feminine. And a true Divine Feminine loves herself unconditionally, no matter where she is in her journey or what she is experiencing. One of the most important teachings of Divine Feminine wisdom is that just like the moon, we go through phases too. Give yourself a break when times are dark, and don't be afraid to shine your light full blast when the time is ripe for it.

THE FLOW OF THIS BOOK

Divine Feminine energy is intricately woven into our life cycles, seasons, and moon phases. There are three Divine Feminine archetypes (also known as the Triple Goddess): the Maiden, Mother, and Crone. Each of these energies is linked to the moon cycle, the seasons, and the phases a woman experiences in her chronological life cycle. If we can learn to work with these energies instead of resisting and suppressing them, we will be able to flow with life with greater ease.

This book is written in a devotional style, but with a *goddess* twist. For an entire year, you will journey along with the Divine Feminine and me, and as we move through the year, you will be working closely with each of her archetypes. Each entry within these pages correlates to the archetypal seasons and moon phases. For example, if you were to pick up this book at the beginning of the year, from January through April, you will gain wisdom from the Maiden archetype and apply it to your current life experience. When the summer months begin, from May to August, you will work with the Mother archetype and integrate her wisdom into your days. And as we shift into autumn/winter, from September through December, you will receive guidance from the Crone as you close out the year.

No matter where you are in life or how you identify, you can always draw from these three archetypes. The Divine Feminine is omnipresent, infinite. This means she exists in all time and space, in all of her incarnations. Because we hold her within ourselves, we too are transcendental, in that sense that we can tap into any archetype at any time. Our Maiden energy can become active no matter how old we are when we travel a new path or learn something new. Our Mother archetype thrives within us as we witness anything we create coming to life, or as we nurture ourselves and our loved ones. When we spend time in deep reflection or mourn a loss at any age, we are leaning into our inner Crone archetype.

The Maiden

Life Cycle: Youth, Premarriage (traditionally)
Season: Late Winter/Spring
Moon Cycle: New Moon

Maiden energy represents youth, new beginnings, and the start of a new cycle. You are in your Maiden energy when you are healing your inner child, having fun, gaining new experiences, or taking a leap of faith, and when you set your intentions for a new cycle. Working with Maiden energy helps you dream big and take risks. The Maiden inspires you to keep learning, ask questions, and develop a connection with your environment.

Maiden energy is curious, free, innocent, playful, magical, and open.

The Mother

Life Cycle: Early to Midlife, Marriage/Union, Motherhood (traditionally)

Season: Late Spring/Summer

Moon Cycle: Full Moon

Mother energy represents creation, harvest, and celebration. You are in your Mother energy when you celebrate the progress you've made on your journey and the fruition of your manifestations. You also experience the Mother archetype when you are embracing your femininity, exploring your sexuality and sensuality, and gaining wisdom from your various relationships. Working with Mother energy helps you honor where you are and think about where you want to go next. The Mother teaches you how to love yourself, share love with others, and celebrate all the wonderful blessings and abundance life brings.

Mother energy is sexual, sensual, expressive, grateful, nurturing, and expansive.

The Crone

Life Cycle: Mid to Late Life, End of Life (traditionally)
Season: Fall/Early Winter
Moon Cycle: Waning and Dark Moon

Crone energy is the culmination of wisdom a woman gains throughout her life. Your intuition and universal knowledge come from your inner Crone. You are in your Crone energy when things begin to fall away so the new can be welcomed, when you see situations in your life from a higher perspective, and when you work through your own shadow. Working with Crone energy helps you release what no longer serves you and create space for the new intentions you plan on setting when the cycle begins again with the Maiden. The Crone guides you through your darker times, reminding you that everything must end sometime, and helping you to see the silver lining in all experiences.

Crone energy is wise, calm, contemplative, strong, nonjudgmental, and accepting.

I've noticed the way the moon affects my mood and energy levels, as well as those of the collective. I've also noticed how the changing seasons impact our mood, motivation, and desires. Transitioning from one phase of womanhood into another also affects our consciousness and vibration, and lots of us frequently cycle through these energies without actually going through the physical and body changes—oftentimes in sync with the moon!

I know you have a busy life, and I know the vastness of Divine Feminine energy can be intimidating. So each day you will receive a small yet impactful taste of the wisdom you are craving—the wisdom you carry within—to ease you into the awakening of your inner goddess. In this way, you will find it easier and easier to embody and live by her virtues.

Depending on where we are in the year, the daily entries you read will change, showing you how to work with the energy as it transitions from one archetype to the next. Having this wisdom will help you understand your individual journey better and will provide you with clear examples for integrating this knowledge into your daily life.

Occasionally, I will name a specific goddess or ascended Divine Feminine and share wisdom from her story. However, most entries have one goal in mind: to help you see the goddess who resides within *you*. We are all connected, and as I said before, the same Divine Feminine energy that moves in me, moves in you. When you come to this realization, you see that all the wisdom you are seeking comes from within you.

This book can also be used as a daily oracle after you've gone through the year. Once you've read it once, feel free to reference it as you please, in any order you like. You may also choose to continue reading it in chronological order as the new year begins to refresh yourself on the wisdom you tapped into the first time around. Feel free to jump around the book as you feel guided to as well. Since the moon goes through her cycle every month, you may feel guided to jump back to, for example, entries under the Maiden archetype when the moon is new while you are in a month ruled by the Crone archetype.

These teachings are designed to help you awaken to and activate the ancient Divine Feminine wisdom within you. Therefore, it is important that you flow with the energy. If you feel guided to jump around, do so. If you feel guided to always read the teachings in order, do so. There may also be days when you feel in need of some guidance but are not sure where to look. Allow your inner goddess to guide you to a page at random and see how the message resonates with where you currently are.

PART ONE

THE MAIDEN

*"There is a woman at the
beginning of all great things."*

— Attributed to Alphonse de Lamartine

JANUARY 1

The Maiden is the first of three embodiments of Divine Feminine energy. She is our curious adolescent self, helping us understand our environment and our connection with the Universe. Her domains are the late winter and spring months, the new moon, and the dawn. In ancient days, the Maiden was a young woman who had not yet been married or birthed any children, but today she is recognized as the energy within us responsible for handling new beginnings of any kind. Our Maiden helps us find our voice and dance to the beat of our own drum. She helps us take risks, enjoy ourselves, and move fearlessly toward our destiny.

The Maiden's medicine is her unique approach to her wisdom. She provides us with hopeful and refreshed perspectives when life seems overwhelming. It is she who inspires us to keep going and seek the new.

Maiden energy is very playful and free, which is exactly why we need her. Let her remind us of the fantasies of our inner child and allow her to lead us out of our comfort zone as we consciously create the life we love.

JANUARY 2

Every day is the perfect day to find alignment within and attract more of what you want into your life. Every day you have unlimited potential and power. Anything you can visualize yourself doing, you can do. Anything you can imagine experiencing can be yours.

You are the artist in your life. In the morning when you wake, allow yourself to dream about the wondrous possibilities that await your new day. Trust that even the things coming from your wildest imaginings can manifest for you in some way or another. It's the beliefs you are thinking and the energy you are holding that control your medium. Have a clear vision of these in mind before you get started, and you will surely end up with a masterpiece.

JANUARY 3

You live in a Universe that aims to please you and does so by responding to your vibration. Your vibration is the energy you hold and put out into the world. The Universe does not register good and bad as you do. Since the Universe aims to please, and provides for you by assessing your vibration, if you are not careful, you may unintentionally attract things you do not wish to attract.

Throughout the day, check in with how you are feeling. If you find you feel low, try to help yourself feel better. If you find you feel great, celebrate that. When we show the Universe we like feeling good, it responds by delivering us more things to feel good about.

JANUARY 4

To create a better future, society must see the divinity in all women once more. On a soul level there is no separation, yet so many women remain divided due to the imbalanced energy on this planet. To change the narrative, begin to view other women from the perspective of your soul. All women are divine in their nature, no matter where they come from or what they have been through. Rewrite any negative beliefs you hold about being a woman, other women, or how society treats women. Honor your similarities, and respect your differences. Embody your innate Divine Feminine energy by sharing it with the women in your life; be a soul sister to every woman you cross paths with. It is time for the sanctity of sisterhood to rise from the ashes and co-create a loving and strong foundation for humanity's future.

JANUARY 5

The world is your playground, and you are meant to have fun interacting with it. There are so many stones unturned and new territories for you to explore; it's impossible to even fathom it all at once. Tap into your youthful and courageous spirit any time you need a burst of energy. Make it a habit to seek out new adventures, meet new people, and try new things. Novel environments are like a breath of fresh air for your mind, body, and soul, invigorating you and ensuring you return home with brand-new perspectives.

JANUARY 6

Place your hands on your body. Make the conscious decision to connect with your sacred temple. Talk with your body, inquiring about its needs and wants. Quiet your mind and listen to your body. Feel the stillness within. Inhale peace and exhale stress. Notice the gentle way your diaphragm rises and falls with your breath. Breath is healing, breath is surrender, and breath is the bridge between the higher part of you and your conscious mind.

When you take time to connect with your mind, body, and soul, you find alignment with your Source energy. You are safe in this space; you have room to let yourself be all that you are. Nothing can disrupt your flow when you choose to cultivate peace.

JANUARY 7

There is a rebellious confidence that comes with youth. When we're young, we believe we are hotshots, and no one can convince us otherwise. As we age and "mellow out," we accept that we are no longer children and begin to believe we cannot be bold anymore.

There is no problem with mellowing and slowing down, as doing so is a gentler way to live. However, there is much to be gained from embracing our inner hotshot as we age. In our youth, we do not have the wisdom of an experienced woman. From our matured perspectives, it seems silly to trot around with such confidence, taking risks for the sake of taking them.

But if we learn to find balance between these polarities, we will find that confidence and wisdom paired together allow us to make waves we never even dreamed of in our rebellious days. We must refrain from stifling our inner, younger selves and instead let her express her passions through the filter of our collected wisdom. Age should not keep us from exploring; it should inspire us to continue expanding.

JANUARY 8

There is value in staying present because every situation teaches lessons and brings wisdom. Whether you are satisfied or dissatisfied in life, there is something to gain. You are always right where you need to be; each experience provides you with new wisdom that will guide your future. Ground yourself in your present moment and simply allow yourself to be, flow where you are led, and pay attention to what your emotions are telling you. Through observation and gratitude, you will find the value in each moment.

JANUARY 9

Feminine energy is heavily influenced by our Sister Moon. Notice how you feel at various times during the month and find out what the moon is doing at the corresponding time. During a new moon, you may feel inspired. Under a full moon, you may appreciate the blessings in your life. And when the moon is dark, you may withdraw into solitude for reflection.

Along with its phases, the moon also transitions between each of the astrological signs each month. The traits of each sign impact the energy you feel as the moon moves through them. Observe when you feel best and when you feel off. Keep track of your body's rhythm and your overall energy levels. Pay attention to which lunar energies best complement yours, and use this knowledge to not only get to know yourself better but to help you plan your manifestations and action steps. Working closely with Sister Moon adds power to your intentions and ritual practices due to her feminine principle.

JANUARY 10

It's okay to take breaks from what's going on in the outside world. This is such a pivotal moment, when nearly everything seems to be a hot-button issue. With so much division and so much information available to you at any given moment, it can be hard to find what really resonates with you. You need time to process everything you are receiving; it's necessary to go into hermit mode for a short while.

Disconnect from social media, the news, and even conversations with your loved ones. Regularly spend a little time in solitude to tune in to your soul. Ponder everything you have been thinking about, and really get deep into the emotions behind your thoughts. Through this process, you will come to better understand yourself and what is true for you. Reemerge when you feel refreshed, with a clearer perspective on the world around you.

JANUARY 11

Whether you are consciously aware of it or not, you are *always* creating through the language you use, both in conversation and your inner dialogue. Every single word expressed is received by the Goddess (creation) and shared with the God (action) so the two can merge and birth your manifestations into physical form. In this way, every word you use is really like an incantation, telling the Goddess and God what you are wanting.

Always be mindful when describing the things happening in your life. Alter any language that you feel depicts the opposite of your true desires, and choose words that reflect what you really want to manifest. It may take some time to totally transform the way you think, but with practice, it will come very naturally to you. Then you will have mastered intentional co-creation with the Universe.

JANUARY 12

As children, even if we were enjoying ourselves, there were times when we wished we were adults. The allure of freedom called out to us—being able to choose when to go to bed, or what food to eat and when, sounded too good to be true.

Now, as adults, how often do we still find ourselves wishing to get to the next good part of our story? We may get bored if things are stagnant, impatient if our manifestations are taking longer than we'd like. Sometimes this distress can be so intense that we throw adult temper tantrums and fall into victim mode.

The higher part of us is always reminding us that there is a process to all things. The "slower" periods are just as valuable as the exhilarating ones. It's the anticipation that makes the manifestations enjoyable. Let's get into the habit of loving both the calm and the fast-paced parts of our journey.

JANUARY 13

Surrender more often to your desire to be soft. The world is a harsh place, and you may have been taught that being sensitive is a negative trait. But your soul vibrates in unconditional love, always. It understands there is a reason for all things, and that every problem you face is showing you how to return to love.

When you shut down and harden your heart, you create an imbalance between what your soul knows to be true and what your mind is perceiving. When in doubt, and especially when faced with adversity, choose to align with the vibration of your soul. There are times when you must be tough, and you will be. But you don't have to be afraid of vulnerability. Embody love and you will find strength. Let your heart be cracked open. Allow yourself to be held. As the feminine surrenders, she also rises in power. Your sensitivity is needed here.

JANUARY 14

Doubt is a normal part of your experience and a harbinger of something else going on inside you. Doubt is fear in disguise, highlighting your beliefs about yourself and your worth. When doubt creeps in, you are provided with a chance to examine what really holds you back: the fear that you are not good enough.

You may doubt yourself, thinking you are not equipped to fulfill your goals. You may doubt your abilities, assuming there is someone out there who is better than you for the job. You may doubt the intentions of others, thinking that you are not likable or you do not deserve love. Nothing could be further from the truth.

Just by being here, just by being you, you are deserving of all that you desire, and you are worthy. When fears regarding your worth pay a visit, remember that the stirrings in your heart are far more potent than the doubt in your mind. When you move in love for yourself, following your inner passions despite the fear you're feeling, you will be met with endless blessings and rewards. Feel the doubt and go for it anyway.

JANUARY 15

You do not need to convince others your truth is your truth. You know yourself better than anyone else ever could. You know your values and your desires; you know which truths of others don't resonate with you. Be strong in your convictions so you no longer feel the need to convince others of why your way is the best way for you. Your truth does not need to resonate with anyone else. All that matters is that you are making decisions that feel most aligned with who you are. People will always think what they think; let them. Be liberated! This is your life to live.

JANUARY 16

We are always provided with everything we need to navigate our journey. The Divine places certain people and things on our path so we can gain a deeper understanding of what is happening within and around us. We may find a film or book that provides us with answers we need at that moment. We may notice signs in nature or hear messages in a song, both of which resonate deeply and reflect our circumstance to us. The Divine is always showing us the way and supporting our growth. It's up to us to become aware of the wisdom being brought to our attention and apply it to our lives. Looking back, we will clearly see how the dots connected, helping us get where we were meant to be.

JANUARY 17

Retire the phrase "I can't" from your vocabulary. You have intelligence rooted in this world and other worlds. You are wise both in spirit and in the ways of human beings. There is not a single thing you can't do. There are no limitations to who and what you can be, do, or have. Stop making excuses. You are uncomfortable because you are listening to everything but your truth. When you start acting from a place of empowerment, you will see what you are capable of. The world needs Divine Feminines who believe in themselves and know their worth. You are the one to do it.

JANUARY 18

Healing requires a lot of inner work. The point of inner work is to explore yourself and come to better understand who you are. When you meet all parts of yourself, it is important that you accept what you find. Your job is not to micromanage everything you deem wrong about yourself; your job is to accept those things and thrive anyway. If you are unaccepting of what you find within, and you are constantly trying to fix yourself, you are doing more harm than good. Discover who you are, accept who you are, and then relax. Nitpicking is not equivalent to progression. Let yourself be—there's nothing wrong with you.

JANUARY 19

When you first wake up in the morning, you are most aligned to your inner being. Activate the medicine of your inner Maiden by working in the first moments of your day. Upon waking, write down the dreams that came to you as you slept. Tune in to your own energy, checking the state of your mind, body, and soul—ask what these parts of you need today. Call in the yearnings of your heart and let them take precedence in your mind. Visualize the reality you are creating for yourself. See yourself thriving as you experience your greatest wishes. Meditate, recite affirmations, and set your intentions for your day and beyond. When you set the tone for your day upon waking, it is easier for you to stay in alignment throughout the day, and it is easier to get back to center if the events of your day throw you off.

JANUARY 20

Clinging to old stories and identities, despite our intuition telling us we've outgrown them, makes us feel stuck. Stagnation comes from wanting to hold on to where we have found comfort before and the fear of starting again. We are creatures of comfort, and when it's time to break out of our comfort zones, we panic. Our perception of comfort and stagnation is really an illusion. We must accept that we have more power than we give ourselves credit for at both ends of the spectrum. We are the reason we feel stuck, and we are the reason we feel comfortable.

Our focus must shift into establishing comfort within instead of feeding the false sense of comfort that comes from without. When we tune in to the knowing of our inner being, we unlock the universal love that is our core. From the perspective of our soul, we realize all is love and that releasing the old is an act of self-love. We remove the chains that bind us and liberate ourselves by aligning with love, holding ourselves as we jump into the unknown. Acting from alignment ensures smooth transitions and pleasant results as we release the outdated and bring in the new.

JANUARY 21

Sometimes others' dreams seem to manifest as if by magic. You may look at someone's success and wonder what sorcery they used to get there. Your witchy ancestors poke fun at thoughts like these. Do you know how long it took for them to make a single potion for one spell?

First, they'd decide what their intention for the potion was. Second, they had to obtain the proper seeds for the herbs needed for the spell. Third, they had to ensure their soil was fertile so they could plant the seeds. Next, they'd care for the plant while it grew and patiently wait for harvest season. Once they harvested the plant, they would then gather any other ingredients needed for the potion. And finally, when the moon was in the right place, they cast their spell.

Nothing ever happens overnight. If you want something enough, you must put in the work to make it happen. You must put the blood, sweat, and tears into your potion—and all anyone else will see is the magic of your spell working.

JANUARY 22

Your environment has a large impact on your energy. Because everything is energy, the vibration of the people you surround yourself with and the places where you are naturally interact with the energy you hold. It's important that your space be clean, both energetically and physically. Things you don't use or things that are linked to heavier parts of your life should be cleared from your space. Distance needs to be created between yourself and people who leave you feeling drained. To grow, you must be in places and relationships that are conducive to your growth. Never feel bad about releasing people, places, and things that are negatively affecting your energy levels or keeping you from reaching your full potential.

JANUARY 23

If you are serious about unlocking your inner goddess and living as a sovereign being, you must get to know yourself. Knowing yourself means gaining access to your inner compass. Without it you will continue to move through life, bopping from one unsatisfactory situation to another, until you finally become so frustrated that you feel like giving up.

You may have the tendency to avoid your inner world. You may be afraid of the things you see within. You may fear discovering that what you thought you wanted doesn't really align with who you really are. You may fear having to show up as your authentic self because you know it requires a heap of inner and outer work.

But this is what freeing your inner Maiden is all about. She is wild; she is divine. She follows her heart's curiosities and won't have it any other way. Free her, and all frustrations will dissipate.

JANUARY 24

The line between freedom and control is thin, and when we activate our power, we must take care. Empowerment feels good, and we can easily become addicted to it. Addiction to power leads to corruption. Our will is important; it is one of the greatest gifts we hold. But forcing our will breeds destruction. Gratitude and the ability to flow take us much further than imposing our will and abusing our power. In all undertakings, it is our responsibility to tune in to our heart space. Are we making choices from a place of love, or are we making choices from a place of fear? If the latter, in essence, we are trying to control a situation. If the former, we are acting from a place of total freedom and alignment. It is love that fuels our fire and brings our desires to life. Fear stops the process, keeping us stuck.

JANUARY 25

When someone doesn't like you, their judgment says a lot more about them than it does about you. You can't win them all—and it's not because there is something wrong with you. It's because the other person feels there is something wrong with *them*. You are the mirror forcing them to look at themselves.

When someone attempts to make you feel bad about yourself, they feel bad about themselves, deep down. When someone mistreats you, they feel they deserve to be mistreated. When people pass judgments on you, they are projecting something happening within them onto you.

Try not to take other people's words and actions too personally. Everyone has their own struggles and hurts, whether they openly show them or not. Send them love and move on your way.

JANUARY 26

It's time to stop thinking small and playing roles that don't feel in alignment with you. An evolving goddess needs fertile environments and room to grow. If an identity of yours doesn't feel like it fits who you are becoming, release it. There are no rules regarding who you can be and what you can do. Handle endings with grace and love. Stand firmly in your authenticity.

There is no need to make excuses about your reasoning for change, and endings don't have to be bitter. Never trick yourself into staying somewhere you have outgrown for the sake of others. You are not meant to be stagnant, gripping on to old circumstances or ways of being. You are meant to flow and continuously reinvent yourself. Allow yourself to blossom in a way that only you can.

JANUARY 27

The Law of Attraction states, "Like attracts like." This law explains that the things we focus on appear in our lives, and it makes us responsible for everything manifested in our reality.

The Divine Feminine energy within us remembers this truth and is always nudging us to embrace the power that comes with it. This power is used by aligning our energy with our heart's desires to anchor them into our experience. We do this by tuning in to how it *feels* to live our dreams. When we can sense the energy of our intended desire as if it were already real, we automatically align to it. This leaves the Universe no other choice than to bring us what we are aligned with.

This is a practice that requires trust in the Universe that our desires are manifesting, regardless of having proof. We must lean into faith and get out of our own way by resisting the urge to doubt and allowing the Universe to surprise us with the fruition of our wildest dreams.

JANUARY 28

You may be hearing the call to rise on behalf of your home and the collective. When you absorb the world around you and think about all the people, plants, and animals, you may feel overcome with a need to do more, be more, and help more; it is part of your nature.

The desire to be of service is proof enough that you have what it takes to fulfill that urge. Go within and come to know yourself first. When you know who you are and see yourself with clarity, you can clearly see others for who they are and discern how you can best be of service to them. Any act of kindness or expression of love is being of service, and you can be quiet or loud about it. All that matters is that you pour your heart and soul into everything you do for yourself and others. Being of service is about being rooted in love and spreading that love wherever you go.

JANUARY 29

You are attracted to fate because your soul remembers you came here with a plan and specific agreements. You form soul contracts prior to your birth that outline major milestones and lessons you are meant to experience in this life journey. Upon incarnating in the physical world, you forget those agreements. As you continue your path, you may recover some of these details. They come through in the form of fantasies, dreams, and intuitive hits.

In this physical realm, however, you have free will. With free will, you may delay parts of your destiny or pass over them altogether. The more you connect with your soul and remember the truth of who you are, the easier it becomes for you to navigate your fated path. Heed the signs the Universe sends you. Pay attention to the things that set your soul on fire. These are clues about who you are and what you are fated to experience in this lifetime. Follow them and you will naturally live your destiny.

JANUARY 30

If you are seeking a new path, all you must do is listen to your inner voice and tap into your courage so you may follow the guidance you find there. Pay attention to where you are being called and what kinds of experiences you desire the most. Observe the way certain ideas make you feel: What lights you up? What sounds good to you? That is the path your higher self is asking you to take. That, or something like it. Start small, but dream big. If something feels good to you, that is the path you are meant to take next.

JANUARY 31

The magic of the Maiden comes from her purity. She trusts with an open heart and mind, she is connected with her inner wild, and she is driven by her lust for life. She grows when she learns the lessons life tosses at her. She thrives when she chooses to live and love freely.

You are her. No matter how life's mysteries have shaped you, you can always return to your gentle nature. You can reactivate your curiosity and chase what enchants you. You can always cleanse your spirit and start again. That is your magic.

FEBRUARY 1

The early days of February in the Northern Hemisphere (and August in the Southern Hemisphere) are linked to the ancient Celtic celebration of Imbolc, a fire festival that honors the fire goddess Brigid. Traditionally, this festival marked the end of winter and the beginning of spring. It is during this time that the land and the people are filled with hope for what's to come in the new season. The omnipresent Goddess energy shifts from her Crone aspect to her Maiden, creating a force that moves everything forward.

The key word for this festival is *renewal*. What is being renewed within you or within your life? What dreams have awoken from their slumber in the depths of your vessel? You have spent the winter exploring your darkness, and now you are prepared to reemerge into the light.

FEBRUARY 2

At the start of each moon cycle, there is a new moon. This is when the moon begins waxing again after its dark phase, and a tiny sliver of light can be seen on her face. As the moon is reborn, you are born again with her. As the moon's light grows, you are called to focus on the new you want to manifest. This is the perfect time to welcome in fresh energy and set intentions to go along with the moon cycle that is just beginning.

From the new moon to the full moon, the energy for drawing your desires toward you is very powerful. If you are setting new goals work with new-moon energy. Under a new moon, or in the days following, you may receive via your intuition new ideas or divine downloads regarding your manifestations. Be open to breakthroughs in your perspective and ideas suggesting different approaches. Act on the guidance you receive to help anchor your desires into your physical world.

FEBRUARY 3

You have likely heard it's best to lead with your head and not your heart because your head operates through logic and your heart gets too tangled up in emotion. The emotions in your heart and the ideas of your logical mind are equally valid.

Your emotions are intricately linked with your intuition, and your intuition works through your emotions to guide you. The reason your emotions speak with such volume is that your intuition is guiding you to move in a specific direction; that direction will serve your highest good in one way or another. When you feel something strongly in your heart, you must act on it. If you don't, you will miss out on parts of your destiny. Not only will you inadvertently avoid your fate but you will also find yourself always wondering, *What if?*—because that experience was meant to be yours.

Listen to both your emotions and your logical mind. Learn how to read what your intuition is telling you about your emotions and how to accept good advice from your mind. Create balance between your heart and your head to be in total alignment.

FEBRUARY 4

The love and affection of an animal is priceless. The sacred bonds we create with animals are prime examples of what it means to share unconditional love with another soul. Our pets see all our colors, including the ones we haven't even allowed other humans to see. Through life's ups and downs, they stand by us, providing their companionship and unconditional love.

Animals are some of the purest souls incarnated on our planet. Their medicine teaches us how to tune in to the vibration of love and express it without words. They show us the gift of being grounded in the present moment, the power of trusting another, and the beauty of pure, soul-based connection.

We are blessed to have such dynamic and heart-driven creatures by our side as we all live our earthly experience. Animal lives are sacred and deserve to be honored for the wisdom and compassion they bring to humanity. We should all take the time to welcome in the life lessons animals have to teach us.

FEBRUARY 5

The shifts occurring on this planet are much bigger than we might initially think. The entire blueprint of our home is changing, and we are here right now to assist with that shift. Everything that has ever happened has happened to bring us to this period of time. We are the ones leading the (r)evolution into a New Age on Earth. So much has conspired just to prepare us for these moments. And now we are here, healing ourselves, connecting with like-minded souls across the globe, discovering our authenticity, and unlocking our power, together.

We have taken on a huge responsibility, and at times our work here is very unsettling. When in doubt, we must trust that we could never mess this up. All that's asked of us is to continue being ourselves, love the way we do, and enjoy our lives. There is nothing else to worry about; our full presence is the gift we bring to humanity.

FEBRUARY 6

There are many different avenues in which your life purpose manifests. You may feel like you need a specific career path or plan to fully live your purpose, but all that is required of you is the acceptance of your true self.

Your purpose is to embrace and love who you are and craft a life that is authentic to you. The real question, then, becomes this: What kind of life is authentic to you?

Living authentically is about bravely showing up in your truth every day, saying what you need to say, and courageously going after experiences you crave. Pay attention to the overall feeling you want to cultivate throughout your life, or the overall message you want to share with others. Start by examining your passions and observing your deepest heart's desires. Focus on that, and the path forward will become clear.

FEBRUARY 7

Our inner child is always within us and appears in our lives daily, whether we realize it or not. Our personalities and behavior patterns are developed by age five. The way we react and respond to things in our world is directly influenced by our early childhood. Whether we had a generally good or bad childhood is not what's important now. What's important now is that we take responsibility for the patterns we developed due to our environment and choose to heal ourselves moving forward.

Our parents and caregivers did the best they could with what they knew at the time when they were raising us. By holding on to their wrongdoings or blaming them for our current behaviors, we give away our power and drain our own life force. To rise, we must reclaim our essence and take our healing into our own hands.

It is never too late to change, but we must be willing to take accountability and put effort into our healing journey. As the child, we had to endure whatever came our way in our environment. Now we are the adults. Let's re-parent ourselves and let go of what's no longer needed from our childhood.

FEBRUARY 8

One day you will wake up and know you have arrived. You will know exactly who you are, and you will feel comfortable embodying your true self. You will feel safe in your authenticity, empowered by your voice, and inspired by your magic.

This is not a sign that your journey is over but rather a signal for you to keep going. Your rising is meant to be wild and unpredictable. Your journey does not have a destination. It is a continuous unfolding of everything that you are. With each lesson, you become wiser; with each rebirth, freer; and with each expression of love, more aligned.

FEBRUARY 9

Nature is a metaphor for all that is divine. If you look to nature, you see birth, growth, and death. You see transformation, movement, and harvest. Nature is alive, and she mirrors you. With each season she brings, you move with her.

Your feminine energy longs to be connected to nature, her wild sister. There is wisdom in her cycles; there are lessons in her dance. To liberate the goddess within you, you must return to your roots and become raw, vulnerable, and untamed.

Toss your reservations into the wind and let your instinct lead the way. Honor the rhythms and cycles of your vessel. Embrace the medicine of the wilderness. Nature always provides guidance, if only you will open your eyes to her offerings.

FEBRUARY 10

You can experience magic daily by living with intention. A cup of tea becomes a witch's brew if you speak your intentions over it (especially if the properties of the herb align with your intentions). A long drive can go smoothly if you tell the Universe you intend to travel easy. A challenging situation can be soothed if you ground yourself before tackling the problem. Anything you set out to do, no matter how mundane or extraordinary, can be exhilarating if you consciously choose to direct your energy and then detach and allow it to be.

FEBRUARY 11

Throughout my life, there have been countless women who have inspired me. Whether it's been a family member, chosen family, or a woman I've never even met before, my heart is overflowing with love for the women whose stories I have connected with. Women everywhere share the sacred power of being a woman. When women come together to learn, grow, and love each other, the world becomes a better place.

Instead of looking at another woman and feeling threatened by her triumphs, embrace her story. Find inspiration in what she has gone through and what she has accomplished. There is so much to learn from those who have come before you, and you have just as much to learn from those who will come after. Right now, all of us, no matter our age, are leaving legacies behind for future women to learn from and be inspired by. Let's set a beautiful example of how powerful women can be when they unite.

FEBRUARY 12

Get to know your own energy and know it well. A lot of times, we feel drained because we have absorbed someone else's energy and we don't even realize it. We may also doubt the possibilities available to us because we have someone else's words (usually their fears) running through our head.

You can easily shift your mood and energy by setting the intention to do so and creating a safe space for this to happen. When you feel overwhelmed or as if you can't move forward due to someone else's energetic influence, cleanse your aura and ground yourself. You can do this through meditation, journaling, or using a smudge stick or aura cleansing spray. When you're re-centered, ask your inner being how you really feel in your now moment. If you find the emotions you were harboring before are not your own, release them into the earth for transmutation. See the energy of them leaving your body and being swallowed by the earth. After you are clear of what is not yours, take another look at the situation you are dealing with. How do you really feel about it, and how would you like to handle it moving forward?

FEBRUARY 13

Energy spent resisting what you don't want to do is better spent being channeled into what you do want to do. Think of all the moments you've spent in your head trying to convince yourself why something you wanted wouldn't come to be. All the energy spent fighting a primal urge that never gives in— for what?

Choosing what you feel you have to do is different from choosing what you must do. What you *have* to do automatically raises a red flag. What you *must* do comes from an inner drive, a fire whose flame will never smolder. Sacrificing your own well-being for what you *have* to do will never bring you the satisfaction that choosing your inner calling will bring, even if only for one day. You are here to live a full life that is authentic to who you are. If something is forced, it's not for you.

FEBRUARY 14

To love another, you must first love yourself. For others to love you, they must first love themselves. Unions built on anything other than love always crumble. Even if the people stay together, they experience their own feelings of despair and imbalance. To heal or attract a romantic union, first turn your attention inward and enhance the love you have for yourself. If you are partnered, show your companion what self-love looks like by solidifying yours first. Self-love is the first step to experiencing the loving partnership you want with someone else. Remember, it's all about the energy you are developing within yourself. If you give yourself love, you will receive love from others.

FEBRUARY 15

The more we awaken our Divine Feminine energy, the more we become aware of how intricately connected all things are. There are four basic elements—earth, air, water, and fire—that are vital to human existence. These four elements are linked with the astrological signs and tarot suits. The days of the week are influenced by the planets they are named after. Each planet rules an astrological sign. Therefore, the days of the week are linked to the elements through the planets and astrological signs they are related to. The moon also travels through each zodiac sign roughly every two days; the moon is influenced by each element.

Understanding these connections helps us make sense of what is happening, not only within us but in the world around us too. We can utilize this knowledge to help us anchor our desires into physical form and release what we no longer need. Working with the elements and astrological energies that are appropriate for our intentions amplifies the power of our rituals.

FEBRUARY 16

A woman is reborn every month, through her blood and her special connection to the cosmos. Her menstrual cycle is linked to the phases of the moon; as the moon shifts in lightness and darkness, so does she. Her magic lies in her natural ability to tune in to lunar energies for clarity, to create and to release.

Heal your menstrual cycle by honoring the infinite deaths and rebirths within yourself. There will be times when you feel full and bright, and there will be times when you feel empty and invisible. If you have an affinity with the moon, you will feel these changes in your energy monthly, especially if you are in a period of transition on your journey. Know that it is okay to accept both the highs and the lows. Each part of your cycle has wisdom for you. Tune in to the energy you feel as you go throughout the month. What is the light illuminating for you? What secrets is the dark reflecting to you? Let your sacred cycle move you. You are meant to reinvent yourself for as long as you live—see the beauty in this process.

FEBRUARY 17

It's okay to take time out of our schedules to play. We're accustomed to pushing our limits physically, mentally, and emotionally in our modern society. We've put too much pressure on ourselves to go, go, go—do, do, do. Although challenging ourselves to push past our limitations can be liberating at times, if we're constantly doing it, how can we expect to perform at our full potential?

Even when we are doing something we love, we can sometimes overwork ourselves. There is no energetic difference between forcing something we *don't* want to do and forcing something we *do* want to do. When we are forcing, we are creating resistance. Resistance blocks the natural flow of our lives.

When our limits are being pushed too frequently, and resistance keeps coming up, it's a signal to make time for play. Playing moves us out of our own way and gets us back in sync with the rhythm of life.

FEBRUARY 18

We are tasked with the responsibility of rebuilding sacred connections that have been lost over time. As our culture explores virtual reality, the call of the wild is getting louder. Mother Nature is screaming for us to find our way back to her—to find ourselves again through our relationship with her.

No matter how technology continues to advance, it will never replicate the sensations produced when we touch the earth and honor our primal urges. During these chaotic times on our planet, the last thing we need is further alienation from what makes us human. We must recall the value of being outdoors, connecting with others, and satisfying our innate needs. To never see nature's landscapes again, to never feel skin-to-skin contact, to never breathe fresh air or feel the sun on our face is a frightening thought. We are not meant to work for technology; technology is meant to work for us. The more we are consumed by technology, the more we lose ourselves. Our future depends on rediscovering our roots and remembering what is truly important, and then cultivating balance between the two extremes. It's essential that we embrace our humanity.

FEBRUARY 19

Life is miraculous. A normal day can transform into the day when your life changes forever. All it takes is one day—one day to see your dream manifest, to change the course of your life, to be freed from everything that was holding you back. But the shift must occur internally before it will unfold externally. You set the stage and the Universe provides.

There are always infinite possibilities available to you. All you must do to access them is decide who you are, make your intentions known, trust life, and be willing to show up for your dreams. Your participation is needed for your destiny to manifest. Listen to your inner voice, act on your instinct, and you will see how the Universe conspires to meet you where you are.

FEBRUARY 20

There is a process to all things, and it's important to remember good things take time. Keep this in mind when setting intentions and practicing rituals to make your desires a reality. If your goals don't manifest overnight, it doesn't mean they never will. If you feel fearful that your dreams won't come to be, look to life in nature.

Everything in the natural, wild world takes time to grow. There is no instant expansion or manifestation in nature. There are rhythms and cycles, most of which are unpredictable, even though they are expected. This is the magic of life; it is organic, ever-changing, ever-expanding.

Indulge in the natural progression of creating your desires, instead of rushing through the cycle. Let your dreams culminate, grant them the time they need to reach their full potential. Savor the in-between moments as you transition from one season in your life to the next. Hold your vision, always trusting the process.

FEBRUARY 21

Everything in this realm is energy. Your energy is like a magic wand. You can direct it and say the magic words, and you can use your wand for both good and bad. The wand will only work if your intention is aligned with the magic words you are using. You can spend all day reciting affirmations, making vision boards, and getting a plan of action together, but those things won't help if you aren't energetically aligned to your desires. Magic and manifestation work best when you're in alignment. If you aren't fully committed—mind, body, and soul—to your desired result, it will not materialize in your reality. Alignment is the key to unlocking your destiny.

FEBRUARY 22

Being intimately connected to the cosmos can make it hard to stay grounded. With so much to explore in the higher realms and lots of negativity on this plane, it is only natural to seek escape through various spiritual practices. Seeing the imbalances in society makes it easy to disconnect from your body and avoid what's happening in the world around you.

The truth is that your light is very much needed right where you are; your incarnation during this time is no accident. You have wells of wisdom and talents that you are meant to share with others. You are here to lead by example, showing your sisters and brothers how beautiful life can be when you tune in to love above all else. Resist the urge to get swept up in the dramas of this culture, while still being aware of what is happening on the world stage. Use your spiritual gifts and knowledge to help yourself and others live a satisfying life, not to escape from reality.

FEBRUARY 23

Surround yourself with people who are connected to Source energy and have a positive impact on you. Your energy is precious, and not everyone deserves access to you. Consistently feeling drained when you leave someone's presence is a red flag. If a certain individual is crossing your mind right now, seriously think about limiting your availability to them.

The people who are meant to be in your inner circle are those who lift you up and leave you feeling loved and inspired most of the time. It is natural to experience a disturbance in every relationship you have on occasion. But if you only entertain relationships that take from you, you will not find fulfillment in your connections. Seek out the people who truly love you for who you are, who make you feel good, and who you enjoy being with. Put effort into building lasting relationships with them and growing alongside them.

FEBRUARY 24

If a dream is calling your name, no matter how "big" or "small" it may seem, it is meant for you. Sure, desires may be passing, but the ones that repeatedly return are the ones worth going for. The eternal part of you is whispering in your ear with these recurring fantasies and guiding your path. Your inner self knows what is best for you and where you will best thrive.

Find the courage to follow the guidance you receive, trusting it will carry you to your greatest fulfillment. Take risks and let yourself be led by your desires. You deserve to live a life that is truly your own. You deserve to call in all experiences you are craving and enjoy them to the fullest.

What you see for yourself is where you are meant to be. It *is* meant for you, baby.

FEBRUARY 25

If you were raised by people who did not love themselves, it can be very hard for you to learn how to love yourself. As a child you absorbed the behaviors of the people in your environment, so you naturally took on their way of being. If your parents and guardians did not demonstrate a strong love of self, you couldn't know how to begin loving yourself. And if your guardians didn't know how to love themselves, it's likely their parents didn't know how to love themselves either.

Give yourself a break if you are struggling to love yourself right now. Give your family a break too. Seek out friends, family members, and lovers who *do* love themselves. Surround yourself with people who know their worth. Do what you can to create a loving environment within your headspace. Remember that solidifying self-love is a process that takes time. The more you practice, the easier it will become. You are here to learn how to love yourself and break the cycle of a lack of self-love in your family. Take it day by day.

FEBRUARY 26

There is a light within you that is always guiding your journey. Sometimes it shines so clearly and brilliantly that it's impossible to ignore; sometimes it's so dull that it seems like it will never shine brightly again. No matter what circumstances may cause your light to diminish, it never completely burns out. It cannot, for it is the eternal part of you.

Your inner light is always there, even if it feels like it has gone. Honor the times when you feel dark, for they help you seek the light within you once more. In every high and low moment, I pray you continuously remember your inner light, allowing its magic to transform you and uplift others. Tend to your inner fires and let them lead your way forward.

You are everlasting light, and you are destined to shine on.

FEBRUARY 27

You deserve to be happy. It is your divine birthright to feel as much happiness as you possibly can every day. No matter what your past looked like, what mistakes you've made, what regrets you have, you deserve to be happy. No matter how people have tried to diminish your worth, you *do* deserve happiness now.

Nothing you have done could ever make you unworthy of being happy. Rewrite any negative programming you have that says otherwise. As a child of Source, you deserve to feel good and have joyous experiences.

Make the decision today to welcome happiness into your life. Release to the Universe the belief that you do not deserve happiness, and get out of your own way, allowing yourself to be blessed with an abundance of happiness.

FEBRUARY 28

Ritual is the very fabric of who we are and is woven into everything we do. We hold the same celebrations each year, we create elaborate self-care routines, and we make our coffee the same way each morning. Our daily practices bring us closer to ourselves, thus deepening our connection with Source. The things we do and the way we do them are pure expressions of our authenticity, and they are what grounds us in this physical reality, while maintaining a relationship with our soul. All rituals are spiritual in nature and provide us with the foundation we need to thrive throughout our journey. Whenever we are stressed, confused, or burned out, it is our rituals that return us to ourselves.

FEBRUARY 29

It is your inner Maiden's destiny to break free from your own inner Mother and Crone, and venture into new territory. The second and third aspects of your sacred feminine energy often try to teach and protect you, just as your real mother or grandmother might do. But no matter how many times your inner or outer Mother and Crone tell you something, the message they are trying to convey won't click for you until you experience it for yourself. And even then, what you endure may differ wildly from what *they* perceived of the experience.

Your inner Maiden remains curious throughout your life. Sometimes you must silence the other voices in your head and let your Maiden forge her own path forward. She will always lead you to hidden gems—treasures buried deep in the psyche—that reveal lessons of the heart and mind to you.

MARCH 1

All life is sacred and should be honored. Everything that is alive—humans, animals, plants—has a soul. On a surface level, we can seem very different from each other. But when we dig deeper, it becomes evident we are all the same at our core. This is because we all originate from the same Source.

For humanity to transform, and for life on Earth to thrive in an enlightened era, we must accept that we are one. We must make it a point to unify, and cease fighting each other at every turn. We all want to see nature's revival. We all want to live happy, healthy lives. We all want to love and be loved. By tuning in to the vibration of love, we can learn to find compassion and understanding for others. Establishing compassion illuminates the connections between us all. When we see others as ourselves and make the conscious choice to work together, we have the power to change life on Earth for the better.

MARCH 2

Imagination is strongly linked with intuition. The Divine communicates through art, writing, and all other forms of creative expression. If more children were encouraged to utilize their imaginations, the world would be full of adults who are more in tune with their innate abilities. Make time to reconnect with your imagination, with the intention of opening to your intuitive abilities. Let Source speak to you through your imagination. Solutions to your problems will come through in the process. In time, you will strengthen your third eye and find it easier to use visualization for manifesting and receive clairvoyant messages about things happening in your experience.

MARCH 3

Magic isn't something you do; it's something you *have*. And you *do have* magic, whether you believe it or not. There is a little bit of witchy-ness in everyone—even though the execution of magic differs wildly from person to person.

Hold space for yourself each day and tune in to your inner world to discover your own flavor of magic. How do you best connect with the Divine? What forms of manifestation work best for you? Becoming a master of your realm is about finding out when you feel most aligned and powerful and using your energy to influence your reality.

Rituals, affirmations, and prayers can help you hone your magical abilities and clearly communicate your desires to the Divine. But the magic doesn't come from outside of you; it is generated within and then expelled out into the Universe. Forcing practices and prayers that don't resonate with you diminishes your power. Find what works for you and utilize that tool.

MARCH 4

You can travel through space and time in meditation. You are infinite, and so you exist everywhere you have been before and everywhere you have yet to be. Through the power of your consciousness, you can revisit the past to heal and free yourself from experiences that still have a hold on you today.

Go into your sacred space, somewhere you will not be disturbed. Get into a meditative state and choose a specific time and place you'd like to visit, or allow your soul to lead you to a moment in your past that needs your attention. Set the intention to allow healing to occur to this past version of you. Approach your younger self as the person you are today and give this part of you a little extra love. Cleaning up energy from your past brings you greater self-love in your present and empowers you to create your future from a new space.

MARCH 5

Your body holds so much information and wisdom that you could never fathom it all in one sitting. Your body carries your emotions, the energies you absorb from others, the things you learn in this life, and memories from your past lives. Your body is always speaking to you. If you pay attention to the way you feel and the physical sensations manifesting in your body, you will find enlightening clues about where you need healing and what is going on within your soul.

Exercise and movement are important because they help your body release energy it is holding that you no longer need. If too much old and outdated energy stores up in your body, it will manifest in a physical ailment or emotional overload. Move your body with the intention of cleaning house. Focus on your breath and allow yourself to release your grasp on everything you're clinging to. This is one of the fastest ways to shift your energy and raise your vibration.

MARCH 6

Your fate unfolds through feeling. Notice what repeatedly comes up for you. Recognize the desires lingering in the back of your mind. The visions your soul aches for are the ones meant to be in your experience. The passion you feel for pursuing a certain path is your higher self speaking to you, showing you where you need to be. Listen with an open heart and mind. Shut out any voice that is not your own. The craving, the yearning, the calling that never goes away: that is your truth—and you deserve to hold it in your hands.

MARCH 7

You are unconventional; you are unique, and there will never be another like you. Your purpose on this Earth, in this earthly body, is to stand tall in your quirkiness, be proud of what makes you different, and love all of you, even your flaws. You do not owe anyone an explanation of what you are, who you are, or where you are headed. Your life is completely your own for you to do what you will with it. To fulfill your purpose, you do not have to have everything figured out. The only thing you need to figure out is who you are. When you know that, everything else unfolds organically.

MARCH 8

The Maiden's power increases as the days slowly begin growing longer in the spring. When the first buds burst through the melting frost, let yourself be revitalized by the new energy flowing in. Allow your imagination to run wild with possibilities of what lies ahead. Dance with the Earth as she awakens and comes alive. Get lost in the sky under the light of the returning sun. Let your heart be warmed by the unknown magic that awaits you in this new season, and let your spirit be reborn. It is time for you to emerge and show the world who you are.

MARCH 9

One of the most thrilling things about your life is that you are always surrounded by plenty of opportunities for expansion. There is always more to learn, to see, to do. By taking in art, you connect with a stranger via the emotions being stirred in the image. By reading a book, you strengthen your imagination, which helps you visualize and manifest better. By engaging in conversation, you witness the magic of the human psyche and recognize the oneness between us all. When life seems dull and you feel disconnected, seek out the expressions and company of other souls. Mingling with your earthly siblings and their creations helps plant you where you are while inspiring you to keep growing.

MARCH 10

As you come to understand yourself better, your values become much clearer. What you value may be different from what another values, and that's okay. Let your values be the code you live your life by. Fine-tune your code—it will be as individual and unique as you are. Establishing your values helps you map your moves. Whenever you feel lost or in need of guidance, turn to your code. Your values will always provide you with a clear yes or no.

MARCH 11

Nature doesn't hold herself back when it's time to shift. She sheds no tears; she shows no resistance. The leaves fall freely from their branches in autumn; the waves break on the shifting sands of the coast; and the grass gets buried under snow. Nature transitions with grace from one part of her journey to the next, letting go of what she no longer needs and creating space for the new to come. As a child of nature, you contain the same ability. Your central source initiates its own equinox, signaling to your heart that change is on its way. You always have free will and can choose to stay where you are. But if you resist the flow of nature, you will struggle to grow.

MARCH 12

You've been programmed to believe it is wrong to be fearful, and that it is a sign of weakness, not strength. Fear is really an alert from your inner being and is nothing more than a flag being waved to get your attention and call you inward.

Fear cannot exist without love. Love cannot exist without fear. Fear is simply the opposite end of the pole where love rests on the other side. When fear is calling for your attention, sit with it. Connect with your inner child, your higher self. Delve within to discover why your fear has been piqued. You may discover you need to love yourself more, or you need to trust the Divine more. You may find that you have some inner work to do, or that a past pattern is showing up for you to overcome once more. Fear is nothing to fear; it is just another way your consciousness expresses itself to bring you back to love.

MARCH 13

When you set intentions, you are planting metaphorical seeds. Each intention requires that you water and nurture it so it can bloom in your experience. To add a little extra magic to your practice, try planting actual seeds.

Find a flower, plant, or vegetable that feels right to you and your desired manifestation. Plant it during a new moon while focusing on your intention. As you bury the seedling in the earth, fully release your intention and know it is being taken care of. Care for the plant as necessary, and trust that your desire is coming to fruition in the physical world as your seed takes root and grows.

This is one of the easiest ways to connect with your desires on a deeper level and instill within yourself feelings of co-creation with the Universe.

MARCH 14

Where we are going, there is only room for love. Pettiness, competition, and hatred cannot survive in the new world we are building. Humanity has been stuck on the wheel of karma for lifetimes, due to the imbalance of feminine and masculine energy. This has caused mass destruction in all possible meanings of the phrase and has left many feeling hopeless. We are being given the opportunity to get off the wheel of karma and move forward in harmony. All souls will be liberated when love is chosen over fear.

Let's observe the trivial and savor the essential. Let's release any thoughts, feelings, or habits of our own that are not rooted in love. Let's choose forgiveness, trust, and compassion for ourselves and others. We can plant ourselves where we are, and align with love; this is how the light prevails over darkness.

MARCH 15

Allow yourself to fantasize; see yourself living your best life. As you lie down each night before sleep, feel yourself there in your desired reality. Close your eyes and let a smile gently move across your lips as you live out your imaginings through visualization. Tune in to the peace and gratitude in your heart for everything you have now, and everything that is yet to come. Your faith in your dreams is what draws them into your life. Having confidence that everything is aligning for you makes it all real. The more you relax and let your life unfold, the more peace you feel in your present moments. Release any resistance you have related to your dreams and bask in the silent knowing that all your dreams are coming true. Everything is always working out for you in the best way possible.

MARCH 16

The Principle of Rhythm states that change is the only constant. Everything comes and goes, whether it be euphoria and expansion or chaos and destruction. At first glance, change may seem that it has no rhyme or reason, but divine timing governs everything you experience. There is no point in resisting change. In some instances, if you do not go willingly, you will be forced into change. All changes occur to serve your highest good.

Your circumstances, emotions, and wisdom change as life goes on, but the bigger part of you remains the same. You are always a divine being having a human experience. And as a divine being, you are always embodying that which is divine: love.

As you watch your world transform before your eyes and you find yourself amid this plane's unruly nature, remember who you are. Dance with the rhythm and let yourself be led. The things changing around you, whether wanted or unwanted, are doing so to align you with love. That never changes—but if you surrender to the journey, your capacity to love will evolve, and change will always be welcomed.

MARCH 17

Beginning a new journey feels overwhelming because we think we have to tackle every single step in one day, for fear that if we do not, nothing fruitful will come of our efforts. Somewhere throughout humanity's timeline, we lost the virtue of taking things slow. We feel the need to force and control every little thing we put our attention to because we are addicted to feeling good and because we have a deep-rooted fear that we are undeserving. Divine Feminine energy asks us to ease our pace and take things one day at a time. As the creator of our reality, it is vital that our energy be well-preserved and balanced. If we want to see our goals manifest, we must be willing to focus on quality over quantity. This is easy to do if we care for ourselves first and ease our way into the new we desire.

MARCH 18

Any day can be a day you experience a sacred pilgrimage and deepen your connection with All That Is. The Divine Mother is always guiding you, pushing you to enter new realms. When you feel the need for expansion, follow that feeling. It is the Goddess guiding you on your path, showing you where there are opportunities for growth.

Feed the hunger aching to be nourished. Set the intention to become closer to yourself, closer to Source, and open yourself up to being transformed. Devour the concepts and insights that fall upon your sacred path. Follow the trail of newfound wisdom. Move to where you are led. Explore your inner and outer worlds. Go and find new adventures, new perspectives, and new vibrations.

You will find the tools you need at the right time throughout your journey. When you are open to expanding, expansion finds you.

MARCH 19

You can spend months manifesting new beginnings, only to revert to fear when they begin showing up in your life. It is normal to have reservations as you inch closer to your desired reality. The human mind tends to overcomplicate things; this is the ego's way of protection from the unknown. Leaving behind what you know—what you perceive to be controllable—and stepping over the edge into the uncontrollable is not always easy, but it is so worth it. Seeking new circumstances shows you that you are not as comfortable where you are as you thought. The desire for more means you are meant to experience more.

Your evolution demands fresh experiences. Your soul knows there is no reason to fear what you don't know yet. This is your sign to move toward your heart's desires, even if you are afraid. Waiting for your opportune moment will keep you waiting forever. When your answered prayers present themselves to you, you're ready.

MARCH 20

Ostara—the Spring Equinox—is a day of balance throughout the cosmos. The Goddess has fully bloomed into her Maiden aspect; the God is embodying his dynamic youth. The two come together to dance among the newly thawing and increasingly fertile earth. Spring has come again, and there is balance between the daylight and nighttime hours. This balance is also reflected in the weather, as the cold months are over, but the heat of summer has not yet matured. This is a period of creativity, fertility, romance, and lightheartedness. As the Earth comes alive again, hearts open to the limitless possibilities of the new season. Work with the energy of Ostara to plant your literal or metaphorical seeds and nurture them throughout the summer in preparation for autumn harvest. This is an ideal time for manifesting.

MARCH 21

On a primal level, what we want most is to love and be loved in return. We want the freedom unconditional love fills us with. The desire to see and be seen by others for all that we are is at the root of everything we do. There is no shame in wanting and needing love. We are love, and it is our nature to be that which we are. But we must examine where our desire for love is coming from. Is it coming from a place of true love or a place of lack?

As we move more deeply into self-love, we broaden our capacity to love others. When we vibrate with unconditional love, it becomes easier to share love freely. Our desire for deeper, authentic love is not innately complicated; our minds and fears make it so. We hold ourselves back from being vulnerable because we fear loving and losing. We fear being rejected because we think it reflects our worth.

Where real love is concerned, there is no such thing as loss. Love is an infinitely expanding energy that always gives. Love is the greatest teacher, no matter how its story unfolds. We can hold on with love, and let go with love.

MARCH 22

Every day can be made special and sacred with intention. Perhaps you have been taught that celebrations are reserved for birthdays and holidays, when every day is a gift from above. Find reason to rejoice in the miracle that is your life, and if you really cannot find a reason, create one. Take time to connect with yourself and Source through ritual, meditation, and journaling. Go out of your way to fill your life with the beautiful and the aesthetic. Light your favorite candles, drink your favorite beverages, and feed your body nourishing foods. Bring flowers home; make your home a sacred space, where you can be free and comfortable. Create closeness with your loved ones through your presence and strive to make the most of your present moments. Speak the words nestled in your heart and be courageous in the expression of your soul.

With conscious intention, open to the magic that surrounds you every day. Rejoice in your now experience with the expectation that even more special days lie ahead—because you are creating them.

MARCH 23

With each exploration you undertake, your inner Maiden is there on the journey with you. It is her curiosity and lust for life that inspire you to reach for more and help you tap into the bravery you need in order to get there. She may be naïve as she starts the process of embracing something new, but she is no fool. Her willingness to learn and expand is what carries you forward time and time again. The Maiden knows that a life spent without risk isn't really living at all. And even though you may feel frightened to take a leap of faith, your Maiden aspect urges you to follow your inner calling. She knows that no matter what, the sheer thrill of it all will be worth it.

MARCH 24

You bring with you the gifts and skills you obtained in your past lives. This knowledge dwells within your vessel, still. To access it, you only need to awaken it. If there is a hobby that is calling your name, or an ancient religion you want to learn more about, go for it. You can unlock wisdom from your past selves by studying the time periods, hobbies, religions, and languages you are drawn to. More often than not, you will find that as you educate yourself on these things, the information you are taking in feels very familiar. This is because the part of you that remembers these studies from past lives is signaling to you that this is for you. Be open to exploring all the things you're drawn to. It is through these studies that you discover more of who you are and what you're meant to do with your present.

MARCH 25

When manifesting, it's most important to focus on cultivating the *feeling* you will have when your desires show up in your experience. First, think about how the version of you who is living that reality thinks and acts. Embody the goddess you want to be, living the life you want to live in your now experience. Tune in to the happiness, gratitude, and love she feels as she lives out her dreams. Carry that energy with you every day, and you will naturally align to what you're drawing in.

Next, surrender to the Divine the details regarding how and when your manifestations will arrive. You don't have to worry about how everything will come together; you just need to know that it will do so in a way that best serves you and everyone involved. Set your sights on creating long-lasting and fulfilling energies, and let the Divine take care of everything else.

MARCH 26

Your essence is your ultimate source of power, and it flows effortlessly into everything you create if you allow it to. It's natural for you to feel intimidated when starting something new, but it is another thing entirely to belittle yourself and doubt your capabilities simply because you are doing something you haven't done before. Cease self-sabotaging behavior, and unleash the force that resides within you. You have limitless potential, and to hone it you must accept this as truth. Dare to dream, and be courageous enough to follow your inner calling. Have such a belief in yourself and faith in the Divine that there is no room for doubt in your experience. Life is what you make it, and you did not come here to play small.

MARCH 27

Confusion arises between the concepts of letting go and giving up. To give up means you are calling it quits. You no longer want this situation, and you are leaving it in the dust. Letting go means surrendering. You are releasing the urge to control how a situation plays out, and instead you are choosing to trust the Universe.

Neither is bad if the decision comes from a place of alignment. Letting go when you really want to quit stalls your growth. Giving up when you really want to put it in Spirit's hands keeps you in fear. Surrender when you intuitively feel something is meant for you, and trust the Universe to deliver. Give up when things don't resonate anymore, and align yourself with bigger and better things that do.

MARCH 28

As you rise from the ashes, claiming your Divine Feminine power, you will face many highs and lows. There will be moments when you feel that you have broken a cycle, only to find yourself struggling with that same cycle a few weeks later. Have patience, and be gentle with yourself. Don't give up on the goddess within—nurture her, fight for her, and allow her to feel and release. Give her the space she needs to grow, and step out of her way.

Her transformation happens gradually and all at once. As is the way of the Divine Feminine; she is a wild force, one that will never be predicted or contained. One day you'll catch your eye in the mirror and see her shining through. You will feel total peace and surrender as you meet her and say, "The journey was worth it."

MARCH 29

When observing imbalances in your life and admitting you dislike how you're living, you may ask, "Is it me? Am I crazy?" As an awakened goddess, you will strive to take accountability for everything occurring in your life because you know you created your circumstances through your vibration. It's good that you want to hold yourself accountable, but you must be mindful in your approach. Whatever you are not changing, you are allowing. It is not up to you to change others; you can only change yourself. With this in mind, the answer to your first question is *Yes, it is you.*

It's you who deserves better. It's you who needs to take a chance and make a change. It's you who needs to express the yearnings in your soul. It's you who is crazy—crazy enough to dare to dream and take risks. It's you who knows settling only brings suffering, while reaching for more is liberating. It's you who is emerging as the goddess that you are and whose life will change as you do. Yes, it is you. You have the awareness to know when it's time to evolve, and you have the power to make it happen.

MARCH 30

Where there are flowers, there are weeds. When you allow yourself to grow and bloom, weeds will inevitably appear to contaminate your soil. Their presence in your sacred garden is only a problem if you let yourself become consumed by it. Just keep rising toward the light, and pay no mind. Be an inspiration to the weeds. One day they'll find the confidence to grow in their own way, in the garden meant just for them.

MARCH 31

At any given point in time, you are exactly where you are meant to be. You always experience everything that is meant for you because there is no other way. Sometimes it may feel like the experiences you want are so far away that you can barely visualize them anymore. But that doesn't mean they will never arrive. Likewise, you may get so caught up in what was that you forget to recognize the beauty of the current moment.

There is a divine timing and order to all things, and everything truly does happen for a reason. Even though your ego may say something is late or an opportunity was missed, your soul knows the truth. Trust the timing of your life and the plan you made with Source prior to your birth. Flow with the setbacks, just as you would flow with the successes. Keep an open mind and affirm, *I attract that which serves my highest good.*

APRIL 1

It is essential that we spend time with the people who make us feel youthful and ignite our sense of wonder. Life blesses us with many soulmates to share our journey with; they come in the forms of family, friends, and lovers. Kindred spirits help us reconnect with our own souls and witness the magic of life. It is their inner light that shows us how magnificently our own can shine and inspires us to let it burn bright. When we let them into our inner sanctum, we experience true bliss and contentment. Let's hold close the special people who bring back our lust for life, and never let them go.

APRIL 2

Energy is everything—what we put out there is what we get back. If we put out hatred, judgment, and the intention to cause harm, we can expect the same to return to us somewhere down the line. If we put out love, acceptance, and kindness, we can expect an abundance of these things to find us.

Everything depends on the energy we are vibrating in, attracting, and sending out. Being mindful of our own thoughts, moods, and intentions improves our interactions with others, and serves a higher good. We can easily influence everything we experience throughout the day by checking in with ourselves first. Making an effort to align our own energy before interacting with others or taking care of our to-do list helps ensure that what we set out to accomplish goes well.

APRIL 3

As a child of the cosmos, you can replenish your essence by spending time under the night sky. Stargazing is an eye-opening experience; it reminds you of your interconnectedness with All That Is while simultaneously providing you with a lesson in humility.

When you feel like you can't navigate your inner compass, let the stars be your guide. Get outside and speak to the sky about your dreams and prayers, even if only for a couple of minutes. Allow the stars to whisper their wisdom into your soul; let your vessel be filled with lunar energy. Let it illuminate your mind and show you a new way of seeing things. Be still and absorb all the night has to offer.

APRIL 4

You don't have to take manifesting so seriously. There is no need to micromanage your moods or fear negative thoughts. Being in a bad mood will not delay the fruition of your manifestations.

When it feels like your life depends on your desires materializing, you may tend to try to control outcomes, sucking the fun out of manifesting. This process is meant to be a joyous experience, not something that brings stress. Release resistance when it comes up, knowing that what is meant for you will never pass you by. Be playful and have fun when manifesting; the Universe loves to see you smiling and having a good time. When you're lighthearted, you create space for all that you desire. If you're having an off day, choose the path of least resistance by accepting where you are, without ridiculing yourself for it. Source is not going to punish you or delay your blessings because you are having a human experience. It's the combination of your humanity and your embodiment of Source energy that births your creations in the world. Relax—let yourself and your manifestations be. They will conspire when they are meant to.

APRIL 5

You are one of the chosen ones, incarnated here with a mission to love and to lead by example as a woman fully aligned with her Divine Feminine energy. You are special and you are needed, simply because you are you. Your eagerness to reach your full potential uplifts humanity. Your willingness to surrender to peace brings exponential healing to all. Your dedication to yourself and to Source instills devotion within all hearts. This is your magic. The more you heal, use your voice, and act upon your intuition, the more you inspire people everywhere to do the same. You are a chosen one here to create a new and better day for every cosmic child.

APRIL 6

You don't always need a plan. You don't need all the answers either. Sometimes having confidence in yourself is all you need. Listen to what your mind, body, and spirit are telling you. Seek out your calm, inner voice among the sea of other voices. Clarity and direction will follow when you make the conscious decision to trust yourself and move to where you're led.

APRIL 7

The child within you is part of your inner compass. The young girl, the teenager, the Maiden: deeply connected with Source yet grounded in her physical reality. She is a blend of both worlds.

She has been with you since you began this life, and she will be with you until your last breath, watching and waiting for you to call on her infinite wisdom. She houses your desires; she shares your wounds. She remembers the blueprint of your essence and the plan of your soul. She sees the potential of what life on Earth can be. She knows the magnitude of your power. She trusts in your creative ability.

Her innocence and purity reside within the walls you have built around your heart. Break them down. Unleash her sense of wonder, her trust in the Divine, her belief in love. Connect with her and give her the space she craves to express herself, and you will know where you are being led.

APRIL 8

Life is cyclical. As we move through our journey, we will revisit familiar patterns and situations from our past. Tests and triggers are thrown at us regularly to help us rediscover the path of our truth. Challenges are nothing more than opportunities to help us realign. When faced with obstacles, we need only ask ourselves how we can move closer to love. This gentle reminder helps us see everything from a greater perspective and helps us shift into alignment. Repetitive cycles and triggers dissipate when we allow ourselves to align with love.

APRIL 9

The Principle of Gender states that all things have gender. Everything encompassed in the mind of Spirit consists of both feminine and masculine energy. To really understand ourselves and how to utilize our inner power, it is essential that we acknowledge these two energies as a part of All That Is.

Feminine and masculine energy are both needed for everything in this time-space reality to exist. Each energy provides us with different gifts, as well as challenges. Part of our purpose during these changing times on Earth is to bring these energies into balance within ourselves. As we do this, we will witness greater peace within all beings of the Earth.

APRIL 10

Release the urge to force things in your life. You may force a relationship, you may force yourself to work a job you don't like, or you may even force yourself to feel certain emotions, when truly you feel something entirely different. The underlying energy behind forcing is a lack of knowing (or accepting) the authentic self. Liberate your soul by choosing to surrender your need to force. Let go of the things that don't feel right to you. Move toward the things that do. Your inner light will always illuminate your way ahead, but the longer you ignore it and stay in spaces you don't want to be in, the harder it is for you to feel your light and allow it to lead. You deserve to live a life you love. You deserve to shine your light. Give yourself a break, and let yourself breathe. There is no true universal right and wrong—there is only what feels right to you and what feels wrong. There is nothing to force when we flow with what feels right.

APRIL 11

The flower poking through the earth beneath the frost isn't afraid of what waits for her on the other side. She knows it's cold, but she is hopeful for sunny days. Her seed has reached maturity, and so she rises into the world. As she is not yet in full bloom, it's impossible to know the beauty that will come from her rising, but we anticipate she will be stunning.

Lowering temperatures in the night make her question if her dream of seeing summer will manifest. With another cold front, she may not make it. She can feel the earth warming around her roots: proof that her goal is within reach. She knows spring is coming, but each chilly night lends her doubt. She perseveres.

Finally, the days get longer, they stay warmer, and she soaks up the light of the sun for hours on end. There are still challenges ahead of her, but she continues to blossom, trusting the Universe to take care of her.

APRIL 12

To live a magical life is to live intentionally, directing your energy in all you do. Consider the colors of the clothes you wear each day, or the colors and symbols throughout your home. Pay attention to the scents you use via candles or perfumes. Think about the health benefits of the herbs in your meals, or the traits of the gems in your jewelry. These are all seemingly mundane things, items and details you can easily overlook if you are not tuned in. But as you start utilizing these things with intention, you will find it is very easy to extend your energy and to influence the occurrences in your daily life.

APRIL 13

Rage ensues when you choose to ignore your untapped potential. The wild goddess within longs to be free and when you suppress her, everything you do that goes against what you truly want adds fuel to her fires of rage. Dismissing your inner voice always leads to greater discontent.

There are times when silencing your truth may seem like the right thing to do, but it is not. Ignoring what you feel and where your soul is guiding you places a heavy burden on you; one that only grows heavier with time.

Your inner goddess cannot and will not continue to sit by and be burned as you settle for a life that is not satisfying you. Work with her to transmute your energy and the circumstances in your life. Remember that if *you* are not changing, you are choosing your current reality. Release the habit to choose the opposite of your soul's calling and allow your authenticity to be the flame that guides you.

APRIL 14

Comparison is a vibe-killer. You can view another's journey through your own lens, but you will never know the full details of how they got where they are. And no one else can know the full details of your story either. You likely have trials you've never spoken of aloud. You may fight inner battles every day, no matter what face you put on for the world. Find the strength within yourself to witness another's journey and cheer them on. Affirm to yourself that the things you want are making their way to you too. Energy is infinite. Another's success is only confirmation that your success is coming. Claim it.

APRIL 15

Your innocence and purity are gifts, not weaknesses. There will be countless new beginnings scattered along your path. The fresh energy and uncomfortable feelings that come with these brand new starts are nothing to be ashamed of. These are sacred markers on your journey, milestones for your soul. Release any resistance you feel toward *being new* at something. One day, you will be seasoned. It takes time, patience, and dedication. But you will get there. Find a way to enjoy this momentary discomfort. It's okay to not know. You will learn.

APRIL 16

You'll know what's for you based on how you feel when you tune in to its energy. When something is meant for you, you feel it with every fiber of your being. Your heart chakra tingles, a smile dances in your eyes, and you may even be moved to tears. That's how you know it is for you. If you feel resistance, as if your body is putting up a wall between you and the thing, then it isn't for you. In these times be honest with yourself about what you are feeling, and trust the redirection. If something you wanted is not truly for you, it only means something far better for you is coming along.

APRIL 17

Life is a sacred gift bestowed upon humanity by the Divine. As your journey unfolds, you will go through varying experiences, some that bring you bliss and some that break you. When times are tough, it can be hard to lower your resistance to the changes unfolding. You can begin to have a distaste in your mouth for life and its natural occurrences. But life is not happening to you; it is happening *for* you. Shift your perspective and honor both life and yourself by embracing the continued gifts life brings you. Everything comes with a sacrifice, and these are always of differing degrees. But as you choose to consciously flow through your experience, you will find that every challenge made you stronger and every blessing increased your ability to love. These are the hidden gems to be found among each gift given by the Divine throughout life.

APRIL 18

Your body serves many functions as you journey through life. It holds your soul, carries your essence, lets you know when something is active within you that needs your attention, warns you, and keeps you safe. Your body is a wise guide and is always communicating with you. Love your body as it loves you. Accept it for all that it is, even the parts of it you wish functioned better or looked different. Make time to be with your body, listening for its wisdom and guidance. Nourish your body through food, exercise, and care so it knows you are there and you are present with it. Release emotional baggage to help your body feel lighter. Your body is an expression of your inner world, and the way it feels is directly related to the way you feel. Know yourself; heal your body.

APRIL 19

All you could ever need is found in nature. Her medicine moves you, frees you from your own imprisonment. Her stones and crystals complement your energy, and her herbs and plants heal you, feed you, and add spice to your life. Her air provides your breath and carries your life cycles. Her water fuels you and keeps you connected to celestial bodies. Her earth grounds you and provides the perfect growing medium. And from her fire, you are alight, warmed, and inspired to forge ahead. Revel in your lust for nature. Awaken your wild side.

APRIL 20

It's not always necessary to be in alignment before taking aligned action. Sometimes doing the damn thing is what catapults you directly into alignment. There will rarely be a time when you feel 100 percent, completely ready for something. You can prepare all your life, but if you never move, your desire will never come to be. Sometimes you just have to jump right in and trust. Everything will play out exactly how it's supposed to. Let your faith carry you to where you are meant to be.

APRIL 21

Our parents are the people who shape our world when we're young. We choose our parents prior to our birth, just as we choose our future friends and lovers.

Our soul journeys go far beyond this current lifetime. We have had many different experiences in our past lives, and we will have many more in our next ones. We choose the parents who will best help shape this current chapter in our journey. Our relationships with our parents impact every other relationship we will have throughout our lives, including the one we have with ourselves.

Our parents provided us with the tools we needed to figure out who we are and what we need to heal in this lifetime. It is our job as adults now to examine what we learned in our childhoods and handpick what we want to keep, tossing aside what doesn't resonate with the person we are or want to become.

APRIL 22

You are here to be a leader of an energetic revolution. As you do the work and strengthen your Divine Feminine energy, your soul's mission becomes clearer to you. The avenues through which you can express your message are endless. Start by being vulnerable with yourself, and then open to what others in the collective are experiencing. There's a good chance that if you are feeling a certain way, there are many others out there who can relate. You are more than capable of being the wise woman these people turn to. The things you have lived through brought you the wisdom you have today. The message you are aching to share deserves to be set free.

Share your story in whatever way you see fit, with the intention of reaching those who need it. Your wisdom will always reach the exact people it is meant to. Try not to worry about the numbers you are reaching; focus on connecting with other humans. Genuine connection formed through our stories is better than reaching the masses, and it is exactly what our world needs most right now.

APRIL 23

Your mind, body, and soul heal through sleep. You take in so much energy daily that you need the sweet release of sleep to cleanse yourself and establish your alignment again. But oftentimes, you may sacrifice sleep in favor of staying up later and getting up earlier to be as productive as possible within each 24-hour period you are given.

Ignoring your body's plea for sleep and pushing yourself past your physical limits is a fear response. Somewhere within you, you may feel that you are not good enough, so you disregard your natural rhythms in an attempt to prove something, not realizing that pushing yourself like this actually makes you less productive. Tell your mind that it is okay for you to rest, and it is okay to slow down. You will feel even more energized from getting the right amount of sleep and gifting your body the time it needs to replenish itself. Your responsibilities will wait for you as you put yourself first.

APRIL 24

The Goddess in her Maiden aspect can be observed through the tale of Aurora, who brings the dawn each day. She suffered greatly when her mortal and beloved husband grew old and passed on, while she stayed young. Yet each day she rises, bringing hope, renewal, and light to beings across the globe. Even in her darkest hours, she stayed true to her path, and continues to do so. As rising Divine Feminines it is our duty to bring the light into every dark place. Standing together, we can help lift every grieving heart and inspire hope within every child of the Earth.

APRIL 25

Rising into your truth and the full remembrance of who you are is frightening because this is unknown territory, but you are well equipped to navigate your personal ascension and the energetic transitions taking place on our planet. Your soul remembers your role here, and it is gently guiding you to the wisdom you hold within. Even though it may sometimes feel like you must do something now to change the trajectory of the path humanity is on, you do not need to rush. Take your time learning yourself, entering your sacred inner chambers, and accessing your power. Every day, you come closer to fullness of your soul through your commitment to loving and understanding all that you are. And every day that you commit to yourself, you are doing your part.

APRIL 26

Your mind has a harder time trusting and moving into the unknown than your soul does. When in the throes of intrusive thoughts, your vibrations take a hit from the words you are hearing. This impacts your point of attraction, inviting more of what you don't want into your experience. This is preceded by guilty feelings for knowing your power, knowing you can manifest what you desire yet getting in your own way by allowing poisonous thoughts to reign.

When you notice your thoughts getting out of control, first take a moment to breathe deeply. There is nothing wrong with you for thinking fear-based thoughts. Help your mind re-center by choosing a focus word or mantra that resonates with you to recite with your breath. I use the word *peace* when I want to surrender and stop thinking thoughts that are blocking me. I notice that my energy realigns very quickly when I breathe and repeat my centering word. Since implementing this practice, I waste less time thinking about things that upset me and instead allow more space for my desires to come in.

APRIL 27

You are allowed to change your mind; you are allowed to choose a different path. You are always expanding. Every morning when you open your eyes, you are inviting new experiences into your life. As you heal and rise, you come to know more of the truth of all that you are. Through this discovery you will find that old identities and old ways of being no longer suit the person you have become. You can choose to move differently.

APRIL 28

You can get so excited for what the future holds that you forget to enjoy your present moments. This is especially true if you are tuned in to your intuition and *know* what's going to happen long before it happens. When you feel strongly that something is going to happen to change your life, you end up blocking happiness, abundance, and love in your now moment. You don't do this because you don't want these things but because you are reluctant to give yourself fully to your present if it's all going to change anyway.

But here's the secret: it's your full presence and enjoyment of your life that guide your path. Embracing where you are and flowing with life are what help you manifest your desires and destiny. You are not committed to living when you project yourself into the future. Life is happening now: Why rob yourself of bliss now in anticipation of what's to come? Try allowing yourself to be happy right now, no matter where you are, with the expectation that happy times will continue to come into your experience.

APRIL 29

It's time we remember who we truly are. We are children of the cosmos, physical beings that are born of earth and spirit. We come from nature. We come from the wild unknown, yet we force ourselves to be something we are not: predictable.

The control of man has taught us that there are rules and expectations we must adhere to so we can be valuable members of society, good girls. But honey, there are no rules in nature. There are no rules among the cosmos. There are rhythm and divine order, but there is no set of rules one must follow. We are meant to be free; we are meant to seek pleasure and joy and do what we can to live lives that are liberating and fulfilling to us. It's time we challenge the world by challenging ourselves. We are meant for more.

APRIL 30

You are ready to evolve. Take with you into your new chapter the experiences you have had, the love you have shared, and the wisdom you have gained. Be excited for the things to come and eager to continue exploring your abundant world. Carry a youthful spirit in your heart, and always be ready to welcome in the new. Whenever you need an energetic pick-me-up, call on your inner Maiden and ask her to lead your way forward. Take risks, be daring, and never stop manifesting the life of your dreams.

PART TWO

THE MOTHER

"Love yourself first and everything else falls into line. You really have to love yourself to get anything done in this world."

— Attributed to Lucille Ball

MAY 1

Beltane, the consummation of the Goddess and the God, represents the peak of spring. During this climactic point on the Celtic Wheel of the Year, the Goddess is solidified in her Mother aspect and the God is rising in his power. The sun is getting stronger each day as the summer solstice approaches. The Earth is alive, buzzing with the rush of high spring. Flowers have bloomed, animals are active, and primal urges are active within every human heart. This is a time to recognize the abundance all around you, to soak up the beauty of nature, and to explore the emotional and physical stirrings within your vessel.

MAY 2

The Mother is the second archetypal embodiment of Divine Feminine energy. She is your creative and nurturing aspect, bringing you into our wholeness and establishing your confidence. The Mother reigns over the late spring and summer months, the full moon, and midday. In the past, a woman entered her Mother aspect upon marriage or having her first child. Today, she is active within you when you love yourself, love others, and vibrate in gratitude, as well as when you enter romantic unions and become a mother.

You can be any age and still access your Mother energy. The Mother is nourishing; it is her love and care that help you expand in all directions. You may see her come through you as you raise your children, nurture your pets, or lend a shoulder to a loved one. You may even find that you "mother" yourself as you grow and evolve.

The Mother is the point of all creation. This embodiment of Divine Feminine energy teaches you how to be complete and how to share yourself with the world around you. She teaches you how to create and how to maintain that which you have created. Her medicine is a celebration of everything you have manifested in your physical realm. Allow her to show you how powerful you are and how beautiful everything and everyone around you truly are.

MAY 3

I remember the first time my lover said, "You are a goddess." I was delighted because I yearned for that validation from him. Looking back, the real reason his words resonated with me on such a deep level is that he was reminding me of what I already knew to be true: I *am* a goddess.

Every woman walking this Earth is a goddess. You may know this, but you might not always know how to claim that energy within yourself, or you don't feel comfortable doing so. The truth is that you don't need your lover or anyone else to validate what you already are. The only person who needs to recognize your light is *you*. Receiving compliments is thrilling, and mutual admiration is important in relationships—but to be fulfilled, it is up to you to validate your own worth.

Recognize *you*. See yourself through the eyes of a devoted lover. You are utterly amazing, and every aspect of you is worth celebrating.

MAY 4

The full moon often brings clarity as its bright light illuminates that which was previously hidden. This is a time when your intuition is likely very strong, and your dreams may be extremely vivid. Record the insights that come to you around the full moon, and pay attention to how you are viewing the things going on within and around you. This is a sacred time to honor your fullness and practice gratitude for everything that has culminated for you. Practice rituals focused on self-love and giving thanks under a full moon, and honor your body as much as possible. Eat well, rest, and take stock of where you are in your journey and where you'd like to go next. Tuck away the wisdom you receive during a full moon and prepare to use these insights when the cycle begins again with the new moon.

MAY 5

The hermetic Principle of Cause and Effect states that every cause has an effect and every effect, a cause. Nothing happens by chance; it is Law. There is a cause for everything that occurs. There are infinite possibilities available to us in every moment. Knowing ourselves, what we value, and what our intentions are helps us decipher what kind of possibilities we'd prefer to manifest in our experience. Understanding the Principle of Cause and Effect reminds us that every action we take results in some effect, thus helping us be more mindful of the things we are doing as we set out to create, and more trusting of the effects of our cause, as we know our actions are aligned with what we truly desire.

MAY 6

Wholeness. To be whole is to accept and love the self. It is a feeling cultivated within that only you can maintain. It is a sacred gift from the Goddess, empowering you to have an unshakeable faith—not only in the Divine, but within yourself. Wholeness is the embodiment of everything at once: soft and hard, silent and loud, vulnerable and protected. When you feel we cannot go on, it is your wholeness that moves you forward. When you are in awe of your creations, it is wholeness that you celebrate.

You are the dark and the light. You are the feminine and the masculine. You are the human and the soul. Claim your wholeness and own up to all that you are. Infuse your wholeness in everything you do. It is the mark you are leaving on the world.

MAY 7

Mothers are the first to demonstrate what it means to be a Divine Feminine woman and operate from a place of real unconditional love. Your mother carried you from the nonphysical into the physical world, selflessly giving you the gift of life—one of the most powerful expressions of Divine Feminine energy there is. As you were born, your mother was reborn and transitioned from her Maiden aspect to her Mother aspect. For these reasons, the bond between mother and child is eternal.

No matter what your relationship with her is like, honor your mother. It was her divinity that brought you into this world and made the continuation of your soul's journey possible. If you are a mother, celebrate yourself for fulfilling the sacred act of childbirth. It takes a truly divine goddess to carry out the rite of bringing new life to this planet.

MAY 8

Infinite in your essence, you incarnate on this planet continually, often with the same soul group. These are the people you recognize before you utter a single word to each other. Something feels different about these souls; it's because this is not your first rendezvous. When you get to know each other, the meaning of their role in your story unravels. Through exploring them, you explore yourself. Like a band of nomads, you move through the cosmos as one, learning, healing, teaching, and rising side by side.

Your shared love is so big that one lifetime is not enough to encompass it all. So you find each other time and time again, lending aid on your respective journeys. The love shared between souls is the force that keeps the world going; it's the real reason you keep coming back here. When you find your tribe, hold them close and cherish how they enrich your life. You have unfinished business and ages of love to experience.

MAY 9

Humanity has lost sight of what it means to love. We've tricked ourselves into believing love is only produced when prompted by something outside us.

Love is the frequency of our natural state, the language of our souls. Love cannot be taken from us, nor can it be lost; it is always within us. Love is the force behind our truth, the core of who we are. We can tune in to the vibration of love at any moment and call on it when we need support or guidance. We can draw from our own well of love to share with others whenever we choose. We are never without love because we are love embodied. All we must do is choose to allow ourselves to simply *be*, and we will find love.

MAY 10

Begin to recognize the ways in which your body speaks to you. Your body tells you a lot about the company you keep, the food you eat, and the environments you frequent. I've had experiences where my stomach would ache from being around people who were shady, or I'd get a migraine when I was somewhere my intuition was telling me not to be. Anxiety can sometimes be your body's way of speaking to you too. Learn your body's language and ways of sending you signals. Your body is always speaking to you and knows what is best for you. Listen.

MAY 11

Being a woman is something to be proud of. The mistreatment women have endured throughout the ages is a wound all women still carry today, and it can sometimes cloud your heart and mind regarding what's possible for you. Although things aren't perfect for women today either, women are making progress as they heal themselves and come together as one.

Claim your womanhood. Recognize the beauty and sacredness of being a woman. Tune in to the incredible force you carry within. Align with your divinity. The more you claim your Divine Feminine energy, the more you pave the way for all women to do the same. Nothing can touch you because you are a goddess in tune with your power.

MAY 12

If you feel in need of inspiration, look to your life and draw inspiration from it. Give yourself permission to be happy right now, where you are. Social media can give you the impression that you must always be doing something, and that if you are not, you are falling behind. There is no such thing as falling behind, and it's not necessary to always be on the move. Sometimes you need periods of stillness when you can appreciate how contented you are and find gratitude for everything you have previously created. Your soul will let you know when it is time to move again. Be at peace for a while.

MAY 13

The transition from maidenhood to motherhood is a sacred milestone on a woman's journey. This transition is fluid and cannot be contained by any specifics. Whether it be a transition that comes from entering a dedicated union with another, the birth of your first child, or the creation of a dream you've long held, this transition is intimidating, exhilarating, and something that will never be undone. You can never go back to what once was, and that's why transitional periods can make you freeze up. But if you remain calm and support your inner Maiden through this process (Mother ourselves), you will be happy you walked through the portal. You have the power to handle everything that comes your way. If you didn't, it wouldn't have come. Believe in yourself and take it easy as you move from one phase of life to the next. There are people, places, and things you haven't found yet that you will love in the next chapter. Flow with the change; breathe through your rebirth.

MAY 14

Your power blossoms when you love yourself. Like the lotus flower blooming through the mud, you are meant to work through your own muck and rise into the light. Part of your purpose is to learn how to love all that you are and to wear your love for yourself proudly. Never let anyone shame you for being in love with yourself. Don't be arrogant—but never hold back from being in love with yourself either. It's the amount of love and appreciation you have for yourself that carries you through life. When you understand what it means to love you, you know when real love is being reflected to you from another.

MAY 15

Minor fears will not block your manifestations. It is natural to fear failure when you are working toward something that is important to you, but it is not enough to block the blessings meant for you in your life. Nothing can ever take away that which is destined to be yours.

When you catch yourself worrying, redirect your thoughts and energy through prayer and affirmations. Acknowledge and accept your fear, but replace it with love to stay in alignment. Your recognition of all that you are, both the dark and light, is what keeps you balanced and aligned. When you're aligned, when you honor all of you, your manifestations flow to you with greater ease.

MAY 16

Stumbling into the awareness that it's time to end a relationship after receiving hints from your mind, body, and spirit for a while is groundbreaking. It's never easy to walk away from a person you've connected with on an intimate level. But staying in a relationship that no longer aligns with you does more harm than good.

You deserve to feel loved and appreciated. You deserve to feel safe and supported. You deserve to be in a partnership that is founded in balance. Any relationship that has a negative impact on your well-being or doesn't match your energy is not worth your time. Know your worth, and never settle.

MAY 17

Intuition gets louder when you allow yourself to be creative. Art, music, literature, and the like are expressions of the soul: divine downloads. You can connect with people you've never met before through artistic creations because they are speaking the language of the soul. The soul speaks no words and only communicates through vibration, so artistic expressions are easy for the soul to comprehend. When you take in art and allow yourself to be creative, you connect with All That Is and surrender to your soul's musings. It is in this space that you can hear the voice of your higher self. When you feel lost, make art with the intention of opening yourself to higher wisdom. Get lost in your creation, and you will fall upon the answers you seek.

MAY 18

The best gift you can give another is your full presence. In today's world it's too easy to take people and the time you have with them for granted. If you want to lead a happier and healthier life, you must bring the focus back to your connections with the people who are most important to you.

Being present with someone is not about trying to fix them or their problems; it's not about pondering your response or the other things you're doing that day. Being present with someone is about embodying love. To sit with another and open your heart to receive their essence is an act of strength and courage only love could invoke. To give someone your full attention and look into their eyes, making a connection with their soul, is a sacred moment.

Be mindful when you are with your people. Put down your phone. Turn off the television. Minimize any other distractions. Listen with the intention of truly hearing them. Show up for them, and give them space to show up for the both of you. When you show up offering your full and active presence, you embody love.

MAY 19

There are so many facets to the life of a woman. We take on a multitude of different roles: daughter, mother, business owner, career woman, friend, lover, wife, and so on. While fulfilling these roles, we also create opportunities for ourselves, nurture our loved ones, and share our Divine Feminine magic with all who cross our paths. With so many parts to play, we can easily become overwhelmed and undernourished.

One of my dearest friends taught me about the importance of balance. She said if one area of our life is not as satisfying as the others, we run the risk of that energy impacting the areas that are flowing smoothly.

It's vital that we always support and nurture ourselves before sharing even the smallest portion of our energy with anyone else. When we are balanced within, it is easier for us to allow balance to permeate all points of our creation.

MAY 20

If we want to assist in the rising of Divine Feminine energy on this planet, we need to build strong, safe, and intimate friendships with other women. Every woman should have at least one other woman in her life she can turn to when she is seeking guidance. When two Divine Feminine souls come together, the energy they create is otherworldly. Each one activates a deeper realm of divine wisdom within the other as they gift each other with their full presence, actively listening to one another and offering support where needed. Each woman leaves the encounter with a new perspective and a better understanding of her own situation. Being seen by another wise woman draws our awareness to our own sacred feminine power. Sharing experiences, stories, and ideas with another woman helps us come into alignment with ourselves.

MAY 21

You always have a choice. At any moment, you can choose to pick the path expected of you, or you can choose the path in alignment with your soul. You can trick yourself into believing that settling when you really want more is an easier road to follow than that of the beaten path.

Choosing to settle will never be the easier path. Every day that you stay chained to a life that is a lie, your mind, body, and spirit suffer. You stifle your own creative energy and growth by telling yourself there is nothing more for you out there and by staying by default in places you know aren't for you. Don't fall into this trap. Open your mind to the limitless potential and possibilities that are available to you. Choose the wild, unknown road.

MAY 22

Your perception of me is a reflection of you. What you admire about me is a trait lying dormant within you that is ready to be awakened. What you dislike about me is drawing your attention to where you are uncomfortable facing yourself.

This concept can be applied to every person you meet but will be most prevalent in your closest relationships. There is so much to learn by observing yourself through your connections with others.

Your parents, friends, romantic partners, and children are your mirror. Your closest companions trigger you to help you uncover what is hiding within. They are the voices of the parts of yourself you have not yet given your own voice to. When your loved ones trigger you, take some time away to consider what happened and why you had the reaction you did. With a little self-interview, you will unlock patterns and blocks within yourself that you didn't even realize were active.

MAY 23

Let yourself be wild. Shriek in the pleasure of lovemaking, indulge in belly laughs with friends, dance under the stars to connect with your roots, and don't be afraid to take up space. Your inner feminine is a wild woman who cannot be contained. Her vitality and essence are deeply connected to the wilderness. Her emotions are the river rapids, her ideas thundering clouds, her passions a wildfire, and her essence the fertile soil. She is of two worlds: the cosmos and the earth plane. Her power is omnipresent. Unleash her through your primal nature and let yourself be fully submerged there.

MAY 24

Every so often we find ourselves looking at our lives from a bird's-eye view, and we ask ourselves: Is this where I am meant to be?

During these times we must delve deeper within ourselves. Why are we feeling this way? Are we observing the lives of others through the filters of social media and comparing our path to theirs? Are we stuck on someone else's two cents about how *we should* be living our lives? Or is our soul trying to guide us to our rightful place?

There is a divine plan in place for our lives, but it is our choices and conscious co-creation with the Universe that determine where we will be. Sometimes the Universe will step in and redirect us if we are going down a path that is not serving our highest good. But it is up to us to notice the signs being sent to us and take the appropriate action. We are to build upon the connection we have with our soul to better understand what we want and where we're being led.

MAY 25

Relationships need nurturing, like everything else. You may occasionally take your loved ones for granted, without meaning to. When you find yourself doing this, you can easily bring your relationships back into balance through your intentions and actions. Show the people in your life that you love them. Do something special for your partner. Surprise a family member with a visit. Reach out to an old friend. Let your loved ones into your inner world and hold space for them as they express what's happening in theirs.

Connecting with the people you hold dear is necessary if you're serious about self-care. You need to open yourself to others to experience love in all its forms, which is part of our reason for your being here in the first place. Relish in the beauty of the soul connections you have, and let your heart be full.

MAY 26

Self-love asks you to release others' opinions about you. Remember, everyone you meet is a mirror. The judgments people pass on you are really things they are trying to understand about themselves. The way you feel about others' roles in your life is showing you something about yourself that you need to see.

People will always think what they think. It is not your job to try to change their opinion about you. Build up your worth, and be confident in who you are. You do not have to prove yourself to anyone. Instead of focusing on what others think about you, go within, and reflect. Your gut will always tell you what is true and right for you. Listen to it above anyone else's opinions.

MAY 27

There's this idea that jumping from relationship to relationship is unhealthy. Although this can be true, staying too long in a toxic relationship is also unhealthy.

The truth of the matter is that the relationship that deserves your attention the most is your relationship with yourself. If you have a good relationship with you, the number of partnerships you have with others shouldn't matter. All that matters is whether you are happy and fulfilled within yourself. If you love yourself unconditionally, you will see that love in every relationship you have with another, whether it lasts 10 weeks or 10 years.

If you're unable to love yourself, jumping from relationship to relationship won't solve your problem, and neither will forcing a relationship that should have ended a long time ago. It all comes down to how healthy your relationship with yourself is.

MAY 28

You are in alignment when you are being completely true to yourself. Alignment brings peace and wholeness; it is an act of surrender and trust. It's not about being upbeat and perky all the time—you are composed of both light and dark. If you lived only in the light, or too much in the dark, you would become imbalanced. Alignment is the acknowledgment and acceptance of both the light and the dark within you. To be aligned is to embrace your emotions, thoughts, and desires, no matter where they fall on the spectrum. It is to act from a place of pure authenticity, not settling when you want more or stifling your desires for the benefit of others. Alignment is to become one with your higher self and direct your life from a place of inner wisdom. When you align with your mind, body, and soul, everything else in your life aligns for you too.

MAY 29

Allow yourself to be held. In the heavy times when you don't feel understood, in the happy times when you are celebrating, in the times when you feel lost, and in the times when you feel right at home. Vulnerability is the real strength.

It's the connections you have and the intimacy you share that truly make life worth living. Be real with the people in your life. Let your walls crumble, and allow your heart to crack open. Truly look into the eyes of those you love. Explore yourself through your exploration of them. Find the Source within each other, and then you will know love.

MAY 30

In ancient practices the sun correlates with Divine Masculine energy, while the moon correlates with Divine Feminine. It is these two energies, no matter how we look at them, that keep our world turning.

Our ancestors observed many celebrations and sabbats that honor the sun and the moon. These traditions are kept alive by pagan practitioners around the globe and are slowly beginning to make their way into mainstream spirituality.

It is important to understand the dynamic between these two celestial bodies, as well as between Divine Feminine and Divine Masculine energy. It is through this knowledge that we recognize how intricately designed our Universe is, and we see that nothing is random, and nothing is a coincidence. We are children of the cosmos, made from stardust, with divine parents, all of us. The traits of our celestial parents are reflected within each of us, and the more we understand them, the more we can grow and thrive on this planet.

MAY 31

It is safe for you to . . .

Say no. Your time and energy are far too precious to be spent on people, places, and things you don't want to experience. Only say yes when you truly mean it. Say no the rest of the time.

Speak your truth. Say what you mean, not what you think people want to hear or what will "keep the peace." Avoid saying one thing to one person and something else to another. Relay your truth in every conversation because it is yours, and it deserves to be heard.

Set boundaries. You are a goddess. You deserve to be treated with kindness and respect. If someone is crossing the line, let them know. Tell them how you'd like to be treated moving forward. If they continue to disrespect your boundaries, you may need to reevaluate their place in your life.

JUNE 1

The journey to self-love is a long and winding road. There are lots of twists and turns and even loops on the path. There is no one map that gets everyone where they want to be, and there is no final destination either.

A more appropriate title for the experience would be the journey *of* self-love, for it is an ongoing, never-ending journey, and one you will be on until your very last breath. There will be days when you feel tons of love for yourself, and there will be days when you're not feeling yourself as much.

Always allow yourself to be where you are. It's normal to not like yourself every single day. You're not doing anything wrong by having some "off" time. Your willingness to keep going and your desire to feel better are your proof that you do love yourself.

JUNE 2

When you love someone, it's important you love yourself just as much, if not more. It is your love for yourself that enables you to fully love another. It is that same love that helps you be what the other person needs you to be: yourself.

When you enter a relationship with someone else, you come together as two whole individuals, choosing to share your lives together. You need to show up as your authentic self so you can grow and build together. Wearing a mask around your partner doesn't do them or you any favors, even though there may be times when it seems like it does.

Withholding any part of your true self sets your relationship up for failure. You form relationships so you can love and learn. Being inauthentic keeps you, and likely the other person, trapped in false cycles. You must take off your mask and let the other see who you really are. It is your unapologetic vulnerability that helps you learn and evolve. Stop focusing on how you're perceived, and just *be*.

JUNE 3

Your sexual urges are perfectly natural, and to explore them is to bring expansive flavor into your life. Sex is spiritual in essence; it is sex that creates life, bringing souls into the physical world. It is sex that creates ethereal bonds between two beings, combining energies in a spiritual union. It is sex that brings you closer to your partner, closer to yourself, and closer to the Divine.

Your sexuality is yet another expression of your soul, and it is part of your magic. Examine the beliefs you hold about your sexuality, your gender, your genitals, and your reproductive organs. Love yourself enough to gratify your sexual desires. Express your wants and needs to your sexual partners. You deserve to feel sexually fulfilled and satisfied.

JUNE 4

The healthiest of romantic unions come from two people who are whole on their own, sharing their lives side by side. Functional and empowering partnerships are born of people committed to their own wellness.

When we look to another to make us feel whole, peaceful, and fulfilled, we unknowingly put ourselves on a perpetually unsatisfactory path. It is no one else's job to ensure that we are always feeling good. It is not our job to be responsible for anyone else's good feelings either.

It *is* our job to ensure that we feel whole, peaceful, and fulfilled on our own. And it is up to us to choose a partner who consciously works to achieve the same within themselves. We and our partner do not need to be "perfect" to have a successful relationship, but we do need to be committed to our own evolution so we can grow together.

JUNE 5

We all have the desire to be of service, but oftentimes we hold ourselves back because we don't know *how* to be of service. Being of service is about embodying our divinity and sharing our energy with the beings of Earth and nature.

Anytime we choose to do something from the goodness of our heart, we are serving the planet and honoring Source. A Divine Feminine goddess gives when she can, with no expectation of recognition or applause—it is her magic. We need not worry about tackling the world's problems at large. We can focus on where and when we can be of service in our community, and that energy will expand across the globe.

JUNE 6

There is power in your breath. When you feel imbalanced, it is your breath that brings you back into alignment. Your breath is a healer and a master alchemist. Through conscious breathwork, you can release what is no longer serving you and shift your energy back to a state of serenity.

Throughout your infinite deaths and rebirths on this plane, remember to breathe. Just as a mother breathes through the birth of her child, you can breathe through your own rebirth. It is your breath that keeps you grounded in this body while staying connected to the spirit realms.

Breathe in to plant yourself where you are; breathe out to release vibrations you don't need. Let your breath show you how easy it is to center yourself in your present moment.

JUNE 7

Regret is wasted energy. To live a full life, ups and downs are necessary. Challenges and setbacks are part of what makes life interesting. Mistakes can turn into blessings if you choose to transmute their energy. Wrongdoings show you what you truly value and make you stronger.

Do not waste any more energy regretting the choices you've made in the past. Take the lessons learned, the love shared, and the joy felt, and keep moving. Keep your values in mind, and take risks when you feel guided. There is no guarantee that everything will go the way you intend—but that doesn't mean you shouldn't go for it. Live for the exhilaration of what could go right. Trust that you will always be exactly where you are supposed to be. Accept that part of being human includes feeling a range of emotions and having a variety of experiences. Some will feel better than others, but at the end of your time here, you will be able to say you had a full life.

Give yourself permission to have a life well lived.

JUNE 8

Sisterhood is a sacred gift from Source. The relationships formed between women who are evolving and rising have the power to enlighten the masses. When they come together, sisters uplift each other, offer divine guidance, and unravel the mysteries of the Universe. These high vibrational relationships bring the gifts of expansion and deeper understanding of women's role in this Universe.

In my life, every time I have wished for a new friend, one has always shown up within weeks. I now have a tribe of powerful women who love and support me. Together, through our feminine power, we work magic to the benefit of our own, each other's, and the collective's lives. They inspire me when I need it, and they remind me of the sheer brilliance that is the fabric of our Universe.

A sister is a friend until the end. Call in your soul tribe and lean on each other as you rise.

JUNE 9

Regardless of what happened before, you deserve to experience good moving forward. There is nothing you could have done that would make you unworthy in the eyes of the Divine. And no matter what people have told you or shown you through their actions, you are worthy of the love and support you crave.

When you feel ready, let go of the hurt others have caused you, and release any pain you have inflicted upon yourself. Any beliefs saying you don't deserve the best that life has to offer are false. Work through them gently, and speak to yourself the way you would a small child. Reprogramming your beliefs is not an easy task, but it is one that will bring you many rewards as you continue.

JUNE 10

Developing independence is one of the best things we can do on our path back to ourselves, yet we should never forget how vital it is to invite others into our world as well.

The toxic masculinity mindset of our society tells us that we don't need other people, that we shouldn't need the support of others—that it is weak to open our hearts and souls to people outside our immediate family or inner circle. Yet the truth is that we are all connected through Spirit. By denying our nature to connect and depriving ourselves of intimate relationships, we are not only abandoning others but abandoning ourselves.

It is important that we be healthy in our independence—trusting ourselves enough to know when it is time to welcome the support of another.

JUNE 11

You deserve every good thing that happens for you. I have a client who once expressed to me she felt guilty that good things were happening for her when she knew so many in our collective were struggling. I assured her she was worthy of the blessings manifesting in her life and told her that her success story would likely serve as a beacon of hope for others. She replied by telling me that she felt that way too, but the guilt still crept in.

When you have such a pure heart, and this woman does, it is easy to look around and feel like you do not deserve what is coming to you when so many others are going without. Shift your perspective when this happens by affirming that you are in fact deserving of your answered prayers, and that this Universe is truly abundant. Believe there is more than enough to go around, and you will soon observe this truth in your reality.

JUNE 12

An awakened woman need not be threatened by women who are also awakening. She should lock arms with her sisters and rise alongside them. Every woman is unique, and so every woman has her own sacred rite to fulfill in this lifetime. There is no need to compete with or exert our dominance over those in our community. If we don't vibe with a specific person, we don't have to hang around her, but we can still wish her well on her rising. Let us pray that every woman walking this Earth tunes in to her innate power and rises. Let us lovingly observe the growth we see in other women. Let us set the intention that women everywhere will come into their true power and speak, walk, and live in their authenticity. Let us empower each other to let our wisdom flow and our love lead the way.

JUNE 13

"Self-care" in the mainstream has morphed into meaning bubble baths and face masks. So many people pose drinking water, reading books, and exercising as forms of self-care. Of course, these things are vital maintenance for the mind, body, and spirit, but they are things you should be doing by default to keep yourself sharp and energized.

Real self-care involves going within and facing your inner demons. It involves setting boundaries, speaking your truth, and closing off your energy to those who are only taking from you. Self-care is about knowing your worth and loving yourself enough to never settle for anything less than you deserve. It's about courageously chasing your dreams and crafting a life you love, no matter what happens along the way. Always make time for pampering and play, but never forget that self-care includes tending to your inner sanctum as well.

JUNE 14

The sun and Divine Masculine energy are one. The moon and Divine Feminine energy are one. Both are needed for life on Earth to be—just as both are needed to be whole within. Spend time in the warmth of the sun to activate your inner masculine. Let the solar energy wash over you and revive the radiance of your soul. Soak in the light of the moon to embody your inner feminine. Allow the lunar energy to bring light to the darkest parts within you. Connect with your celestial parents when you need support and guidance. They will always ignite the infinite wisdom you hold within you.

JUNE 15

The word *feminine* may conjure certain images in your mind that when you really think about them, make you feel caged in. This response likely comes from what society expects a feminine woman to be like versus how you perceive feminine energy to be.

The feminine is a creatrix; this means she has the power to concoct anything her heart desires, including how she exudes her own sacred energy. It's essential that you define what the omnipresent Divine Feminine and your own inner feminine mean to you. Understanding how you perceive feminine power helps you craft yourself and your life to your liking. By honoring your unique magic, you own the fact that your experience is for you and no one else. You can drop the pressure to downplay your own desires in the name of what anyone else expects from you, and you are free to explore every avenue your heart is pulling you toward.

JUNE 16

Freedom is a driving force that everyone wishes to obtain. But freedom is not something that can be chased; it is a sensation that must be drawn out from within. To be free is to revel in the essence of you, to understand and love yourself to such an extent that there is nothing left in your experience to encumber you. It is the reckoning of all that held you back before, the destruction of false constructs that have weighed on you for too long. It's the culmination of all that you are, pulsating through your veins. The truth of who you are, the unfeigned and the uncontrollable aspects of you.

Dive into your love affair with freedom. Let it transform you into the wild goddess you are meant to be, the wild goddess you are. Get tangled up in its rawness, but give it space to be itself. When you unite with freedom, codependency dies and sovereignty thrives. You can never go back to who you were before; freedom is a part of you.

JUNE 17

Celebrate the progress you have made on your journey. You are not the same person you were yesterday, and you are not the person you will be tomorrow. All you have is your present moment, and each day provides more opportunities for growth and expansion.

Praise yourself for the inner work you have done, the shadows you've illuminated, and the truths you've unveiled. Every day you are loving yourself a little more and aligning with the life you've always dreamed of. Even on the days that weren't the easiest, you pulled through. And here you are, radiant and eager to shine.

Celebrate you, today and every day. You deserve it.

JUNE 18

Maintaining your relationship with Source is equally as important as maintaining your most intimate relationships, or the relationship you have with yourself. Source is your partner in life, and you've got to water this relationship just as you would any other. You wouldn't expect your partner to always put more work into your union than you—so why would you expect Source to put in 70 percent when you're only giving 30 percent?

Bring balance into your connection with Source through ritual and meditation, by being grateful and shining your light. Share love wherever you go, work on yourself, and transmute fear-based thoughts into loving ones. As you do this, Source will be ready to support you in all you need. Source energy wants nothing more than to see you thriving, acting as a beacon of light, and living your best life.

JUNE 19

Our Universe is abundant, and there is more than enough to go around for everyone. Understand that what you allow into your experience is what comes through. Open up your ability to receive more, and more will surely come. Don't shut off your receptivity by hanging on to feelings of jealousy or comparison. Relax into the knowing that the things meant for you will always make their way to you. Make room for greater abundance by showing gratitude for everything you already have. Know that when someone else wins, they are not taking anything away from your blessings, and vice versa. You are an alchemist, and energy grows where your attention flows.

JUNE 20

Make the commitment to be as supportive of yourself as you are of those you love. You may be willing to encourage your children, friends, and lovers to chase their dreams, but are at a loss for words when in need of that support yourself.

Channel the encouragement you give to others in your own direction too. Your ideas and aspirations are just as worthy as anyone else's. You deserve the things you desire, and you deserve support and encouragement as well. Lift yourself up and inspire through your example.

JUNE 21

The summer solstice, or Litha, the longest day and shortest night of the year, comes at the peak of Mother season each summer. This day is dedicated to the life-giving power of the sun and honors the omnipresent Divine Masculine. This sacred celebration on the Wheel of the Year observes the beauty and abundance of the earth.

The sun and the God are at their peak strength, and the days, as well as the God, will slowly fade away until Yule time when they are reborn again. The Goddess is pregnant with the new God, who will be birthed in the winter. Love vibrations are high at midsummer; the romance blossoming between these two cosmic lovers can be felt within every heart.

Utilize the magic of this sabbat by uniting your inner feminine and inner masculine energies. Create with your goddess and act with your god. Take stock of where you are in your journey. What has manifested for you since the beginning of the year? What would you like to see manifest before the year's end? Practice rituals dedicated to your goals, and follow up with empowered action in your physical world.

JUNE 22

Your magic comes from your authenticity and your sexual energy. Your authenticity is your core, and your sexuality is the expression of your core. Sexual energy is more than what is generated in the act of lovemaking. It is your unique life-force energy, the mother of creation. When you combine the blueprint of your soul with expression in the physical world, you bring forth the manifestation of your wildest imaginings.

To work with this magic, first get to know yourself. Create intimacy within your own depths. Learn yourself: the way you move, the way you trust, the way you love. Understand all that you are, and you will naturally discover your sexual energy. Let it awaken and rise to the surface. Your unapologetic self-expression is the power that births worlds.

JUNE 23

Energy speaks volumes over words. Whether you're observing the energy of yourself or someone or something outside you, everything you need to know can be found in the energy. Pay attention to the vibration you feel coming from a person, place, or thing. Notice the different energies you pick up on wherever you go each day. Reading energy is a major part of your intuition. Developing this practice will help you fine-tune your intuitive abilities.

JUNE 24

Soul-to-soul attraction is on another level from physical attraction. Feeling a magnetic pull to another is a sign from your higher self that you recognize this soul from a previous lifetime, and that you may share a soul contract that both of you are fated to honor in this lifetime.

Soul attraction is undeniable and uncontrollable. The energy vibrating between two souls who are meant to share an experience is all-encompassing, with almost sexual notes, even if the relationship is platonic. It is nearly impossible to ignore the desire to get to know the other soul, whether you intend to pursue friendship, a romantic relationship, or a professional partnership with them. This is a surefire sign that you and this person have spiritual business to attend to. Don't worry about trying to figure it out. Align with your authenticity and flow where the energy takes you. Whatever you experience together will help shape your life.

JUNE 25

You can only experience as much intimacy with others as you have created within yourself. Facing the reality of your feelings can be frightening because you know that you will have to make changes in your life in response to what you feel. Change is not always easy, but it is one of the only constants on this plane. If you do not allow yourself to change, you block the blessings, opportunities, and abundance that are destined for you.

Be honest with yourself. Cultivate that trust and that safety within yourself first. Don't be afraid to examine each corner of your conscious and subconscious minds. Knowing yourself allows others to know the real you.

JUNE 26

Loving yourself means much more than admiring the way you look or treating yourself to spa days. Loving yourself is about knowing your worth: knowing when you deserve better and making changes accordingly.

Loving yourself means standing up for yourself and enforcing your boundaries. It means speaking your truth and following up with actions to walk your talk. Loving yourself only on a surface-level basis will not suffice. Dig a little deeper, and love the nitty-gritty. That's when the real magic happens.

JUNE 27

You are not here to fit into some mold that was created for you before your conception. You are here to forge your own path forward, in your own unique way. You can be anyone you want to be. You can live however you want to live. The only person you must answer to is yourself. No one else has any right to say what you should be doing with your time or what kind of path you should follow. Put your own opinions and your own desires above those of others. Be honest with yourself. Let opposition fuel your inner fire, and walk away from all that doesn't resonate with grace. You are the mother, the child, and the old wise woman—it all comes down to you. What kind of life do you want to live?

JUNE 28

At the core of your being lies your truth. Your truth is composed of the things you have experienced since your soul's genesis, including your current incarnation. Your truth houses your soul's plan and is the force directing your life.

Like your intuition, your truth comes through subtly, yet with a strong resonance. What is true for you feels like an inner knowing. Your truth resonates on such a deep level that when you come upon it, you feel like you are finally home. Embracing your truth brings total liberation and unconditional self-love.

Speaking and living your truth require the unapologetic embodiment of your authentic self. When you live in truth, you are not projecting from your insecurities or manipulating your fears. When you live in truth, you are showing up raw—no masks, no walls, no denial. Living your truth means you are no longer a parody of yourself, a taste of what could be. Living your truth means you are living in a way only you can and crafting a life you love: a bona fide goddess who knows her worth.

JUNE 29

Extend a hand to others. The entire planet is being upgraded on an energetic level, and humanity is evolving. This journey is not easy, and it is not over yet. You know how difficult it has been for you. Keep this in mind when someone snaps at you in the grocery store or is short with you on a call. Everyone is feeling the effects of the planet's ascension, and everyone processes their personal ascension differently. If you are serious about your own evolution, as well as the evolution of the planet, lend a hand. Be patient with the people you meet, and hold space for the ones in your circle having a rough time. Meet people where they are, and offer love. That is all that's required of you.

JUNE 30

Your energy is precious and should be protected. Not everyone deserves access to your essence. You do not need to feel guilty for cutting off people and things that are negatively impacting your energy. You can end relationships and set boundaries with clear, concise communication. There is no need to overexplain your decisions. Let others know where you are coming from clearly, without making excuses or apologizing. You have the right to change your mind and protect yourself, and you must always do what is best for you.

JULY 1

You are a queen, a goddess. You are royalty. The sooner you realize this, the sooner you will rise and claim your throne. You are here to be a leader of the spiritual revolution by activating and utilizing your Divine Feminine power. When in doubt, tune in to your heart space. Find a mirror and gaze into your own eyes. Draw inspiration from the depths of your own suffering and your own peace. You have wells of wisdom within you, waiting for you to drink from them. You are a divine spark of light, an expanding fragment of All That Is. Everything happening in the Universe is conspiring in your favor. You are always being led down the path of your highest good. Trust and accept that you are meant to rule.

JULY 2

Every relationship you have is meant for you. Every person you develop a relationship with, no matter how long it lasts or whether it is generally positive or negative, is meant to be in your experience at that time. People come in and out of your life—some are in the main cast and some are only guest stars, but all fill powerful supporting roles.

If you develop a relationship with someone, there is a reason for their presence in your life. They may have something new to teach you, or they may help you recognize something happening within you that you didn't see before. Whatever the reason, all relationships you have bring you something valuable and help you grow into who you're meant to be.

JULY 3

There is a difference between your purpose and what you came here to do. You are made from Source energy. Source energy is love. You are here to remember where you came from and share that wisdom with others. Your purpose is to embody love.

What you came here to do varies wildly. You may have come here to be, do, have, and experience many things. You will play many different roles throughout your life cycle. But the most important one you will ever play involves remembering your essence and sharing it with others.

JULY 4

Embodying your inner Mother aspect does not require you to become a mother to a child, although it can certainly mean that. Your Mother energy is active within you when you are nurturing and loving yourself, sharing your life with a special someone, or providing a shoulder for a friend to cry on. You can tune in to your Mother aspect by doing things you love to do and practicing the virtue of patience, as you create the projects and life of your dreams. You can activate your Mother aspect by combining your inner masculine and inner feminine energies to manifest your desires into physical reality. Everything you dream up that comes to be is a result of the power of your Mother aspect.

JULY 5

Self-love comes down to a simple truth: you matter. When it comes to self-love, it's not necessary that you feel *in love* with yourself all the time. What's important is that you recognize you matter, whether you are happy with yourself today or not.

You matter, always. Your thoughts matter, your feelings matter, and your opinions matter. Your dreams matter, your needs matter, and your voice matters. On your good days, on your bad days, when someone mistreats you, when you make mistakes, you matter. As you win, as you lose, in change, and in stagnation, you always matter.

Accept this as truth, and unconditional self-love behavior happens naturally.

JULY 6

Check yourself regularly. Observe how you're moving. Consider your actions, commitments, and roles.

A person dedicated to themselves and their growth expands at a fast pace. It is natural to begin feeling as if some of your commitments no longer resonate with the person you are becoming. When you begin to feel off, it's usually because you are denying some part of your truth. Reevaluate your situations. Release the people, habits, interests, or places that are linked to an outdated version of yourself. You are allowed to put an end to previous engagements and ways of being. You are allowed to change and take up space. Trust your inner knowing to tell you when it's time to move differently, and make haste. Staying somewhere you have outgrown will always be unfulfilling.

JULY 7

Forgiveness is freedom's counterpart. Perhaps you tend to resist forgiveness, deeming the recipient of it undeserving. Until you surrender to forgiveness, you will remain chained to the past.

When you forgive, you are forgiving for *yourself*, not the other people involved. By choosing forgiveness, you are not saying, "What you did to me was okay." You are saying, "I will not allow this to have power over me anymore."

Lean into your bitterness for a little while to honor your darkness. Then make the conscious decision to forgive and rise into the light, freeing yourself from the pain of the past.

JULY 8

Everything starts and ends with you. Society may have shown you to play the role of the victim and point fingers when you feel unhappy instead of looking within yourself. No one else has power over you; only you have power over you. Your suffering is not inflicted by the circumstances in your life. Your suffering comes from your inability to trust yourself and recognize your worth.

Get to know the real you. Discover the meaning behind your triggers—don't just label them and call it a day. Understand why you feel the way you do before blaming the situations in your life. True happiness and fulfillment come from establishing your own wholeness. When in doubt, switch your focus back to you, and clarity will always follow.

JULY 9

The Principle of Mentalism proposes that Spirit is the Creator of All, and we (all of life) and the whole of the Universe live within the mind of Spirit.

Everything that exists is a thought of Spirit; everything is Spirit expressing itself. We are all connected because we originated from the same source. I believe this is why certain gods and goddesses from varying cultures have a very similar counterpart in another culture. Think of Aphrodite and

Venus, for example: two very similar goddesses from different cultures. And we will find this throughout all religions and spiritual practices, just as we will connect with friends whose circumstances mirror ours.

We are all divine because we all come from divinity. The only thing separating us from each other and from Spirit is our own programming.

JULY 10

We believe it is noble to sacrifice our well-being for that of another. When we love to our full capacity, we want to be, do, and have everything our loved ones need. It's only natural to want to do all we can for the special people in our lives, but when we are doing so at the sake of our own wishes and wellness, we are not doing anyone any good.

Stifling our desires in favor of people pleasing leads to habitually displeasing circumstances and hindrances in our journey. Our needs are just as important and our wants just as valid as those of our loved ones. When we don't allow ourselves to express these, we wind up resenting the people we have sacrificed so much for.

Through the awakening power of self-love, we will come to realize our worth. As we accept that we are worthy, we will find it increasingly difficult to say no to ourselves and much easier to say no to others.

JULY 11

Inner union between your own feminine and masculine energy must occur before you can fully surrender to true love. By developing your feminine and masculine energy, you come to really know who you are and create wholeness within. When you feel whole, you can fully surrender to another because there is no question in your mind about who you are. There is no need to control, or hide behind a mask; all that's required of you is your presence. As you let yourself simply *be*, you will shift into new levels and deeper understandings of what it means to truly be united with another. Each of you is whole and each of you is independent, yet you come together in the most beautiful way to share your lives as one, all because you nurtured yourself first, creating love from within.

JULY 12

Time is only an illusion, so it can never be wasted. When we surrender our attachment to the timing of our lives, we gift ourselves the ability to flow.

We are always given what we need when we need it. We are always right where we need to be, at any moment. We are never missing out on anything because what is meant for us always finds us. There is a process to all things, and as we tune in to the messages of our soul, we naturally become aware of the cycles and lessons playing out for us. When we ground ourselves in our present moments and commit to our healing, we move through our lessons with less resistance. As we learn what we need to learn, and heal what we need to heal, life keeps flowing. This is the symbiotic cosmic dance happening between us and life.

JULY 13

The desire to control situations sneaks up on us without our realizing it. If we withhold our true feelings, we are controlling. If we say something that isn't true, we are controlling. If we take an action we don't want to take in order to please another, we are controlling. Sometimes our control feels completely justified. But we must remember that any time we aim to control, we dip into our toxic feminine energy. Foundations built on toxicity never last. For longevity, we need to focus on authentic speech, actions, and expressions. Anything that crumbles under the power of our authenticity is not meant to stay in our experience anyway.

JULY 14

Meet yourself where you are. Whatever you are feeling is okay for you to feel. You don't have to compare yourself or your journey to anyone else's. There is no scorecard. No one is keeping track of your progress, your setbacks, your accomplishments, or your failures. Honor the space you are in. Sit with your thoughts and emotions. Use them to fuel your determination, and try again tomorrow. Look at things that haven't worked out as redirection from the Divine. Celebrate everything you make happen, even if it is something you perceive to be small. Every day you are here doing the damn thing is a day to be proud of yourself.

JULY 15

When manifesting, it's necessary to tap into the overall feeling of what you are calling into your reality. The same can be said for the act of surrendering. It's one thing to claim surrender, but it's another thing entirely to really mean it.

If you find yourself constantly thinking about the thing you are surrendering, then you haven't surrendered. Not really. I am not saying this to make you feel bad; I just want you to be aware, as this is something I have dealt with many times. The art of surrender is an energetic shift within your mind and body. You will know when you have fully surrendered because you will feel the change in your own energy and heart.

There's no need to berate yourself if you're struggling to fully surrender. As with anything else, take it one day at a time. Recall the truth that everything in your experience is something you are meant to learn from. If it's still active within you, you are still learning from it. Give yourself a break and allow yourself to move into surrender; don't force it. You'll shift into surrender with little effort when the time is right.

JULY 16

The power of self-love makes you glow differently. As you honor yourself by accepting all that you are, your aura expands. Like Persephone rising from the underworld, you take on a new form, breathing life into what has died and transmuting it into something new. The sparkle of your soul twinkles in your eyes, shimmers on your skin, and dances on your hair. Your vibrant energy radiates outward and works its magic on every being you encounter. Loving yourself is the best thing you can do for yourself and everyone else. Be unapologetic with your glow.

JULY 17

Real connection is born of people who aren't afraid to be raw, to dig beneath the surface and reveal their innermost selves to each other. To crack open and allow authenticity to pour from their vessel. Intimacy comes from the willingness to communicate the deepest parts of our being. The only thing more freeing than being real with ourselves is being real with others. Let's normalize creating safe spaces for ourselves and the people in our lives to express our souls. Pure liberation and unconditional love are the grand revolution.

JULY 18

Prosperity is an energy, just like everything else in this realm. You can attune your energy to match the frequency of abundance you want to welcome into your life. Begin by addressing your relationship to money, resources, and the financial flow of your life. Examine the thoughts you hold about money. Do your beliefs about money support or impede the flow of prosperity in your experience? How can you open your energy to allow more money to come in?

Money is not evil. It is your divine birthright to live in an abundance of everything you could ever want or need, and money is no different. See money as the energy that it is—an energy that you can interact with, one that requires as much work and effort as all your other relationships do. There needs to be a balance of giving and receiving, there needs to be respect, and there needs to be trust. Establish this, and you will find that money comes to you consistently.

JULY 19

The boundaries we put in place apply as much to us as they do to others. What good would our boundaries be if we expected others to honor them but we ourselves did not uphold them? Setting boundaries for ourselves is a protective form of self-care. When we know we are doing something that is not good for us, and we consciously decide to stop it, holding that promise to ourselves is very important. After all, we have to look out for ourselves. We have to hold ourselves accountable. We are the only person we will journey through this entire life experience with. Let's be friends to ourselves and respect our own boundaries.

JULY 20

A win for one woman is a win for all women. Your success affects women you don't even know are watching you. As you rise into your full potential, you empower other women to do the same. As you pour into the pool of the sacred feminine, you nourish your sisters, activating not only their desire to rise but their knowing that they can. The energy you exude as you liberate yourself and reach your full potential comes back to you tenfold when other women do the same.

So when you feel alone, or when you feel that your path is too challenging, remember that you have soul sisters all over the planet who are rooting for you. Move forward fearlessly, knowing that your wins are for women everywhere. And when you witness another woman rising, celebrate with her. There is no need to feel threatened by another woman's growth and success, for she wins for you too.

JULY 21

Get comfortable receiving compliments without diverting the attention away from yourself or shying away. Words of love and empowerment are included in the abundance the Universe wishes to deliver to you. By pushing compliments away, you are denying your own worth and your birthright to receive riches.

When someone says something nice, say thank you. Own it! Show the Universe you know your value and intend to attract what you deserve.

JULY 22

Self-love has risen in popular culture, which is amazing to witness, but remember that sharing genuine love with another can be just as powerful. Self-love is not meant to replace the love you share with the people in your life; it is meant to enhance it.

It's wonderful to be independent and know who you are. It's important that you fulfill yourself and are whole on your own. But self-love cannot replace your relationships. You're here to unveil your own rawness and expose yourself to the vastness of others, to broaden your awareness of what it means to *really love*.

Negating the importance of connection with others defeats the purpose of your incarnation. Open your heart and let love in.

JULY 23

Your sexual power is just as potent as the power of your mind (if not more so). Sexual energy creates all life, brings divine counterparts into union, and moves your physical world forward. When your sexual energy is dormant, you become lethargic. And when your sexual energy is awake, it blazes through your body like a wildfire, setting you alight with passion and determination.

People think working magic comes from convoluted rituals and howling at the moon at midnight. And although those things can help, they are certainly not the only ways to tune in to your Goddess-given abilities. Your life force and your sexual energy are what set any spell work up for success. Start infusing your manifestations with sexual energy, and witness how everything in your experience comes back to life when you do.

JULY 24

Honor the men who are showing up in their Divine Masculine energy, following their hearts, and helping lead humanity into its divinity. Yes, there are men in the world who are wounded and as a result have hurt others, especially women. But there are also wounded women in the world who have hurt others, including men. As you heal yourself and your relationships with women, you must also heal your relationships with and your ideas about men. Every person on this planet deserves love, regardless of their actions and mistakes. If someone has hurt you, recognize they are wounded and send them healing energy when you are ready. Their wounds do not excuse the harm they have inflicted upon you, but this shift in perspective can help you heal and rise.

Love the men who are truly present in your life, whether they be your partner, your father, your sons, or others. It is your Divine Feminine energy that helps them come into their Divine Masculine power. Inspire them, guide them, and encourage them. Our planet needs aligned and powerful men just as much as it needs aligned and powerful women.

JULY 25

You are not meant for everyone, nor should you try to be. There is nothing more attractive than living freely in your truth. If someone doesn't resonate with the vibe you're providing, let them go their own way. Shrinking yourself to fit into a place where you're not meant to be is detrimental not only to you but to everyone else involved. Operating under a façade to please others is draining and blocks your blessings from coming through. Put emphasis on your growth, and let yourself soar to new heights. The right people will always find you and be there to cheer you on when you stand proudly as your authentic self.

JULY 26

Marriage between our inner sacred feminine and sacred masculine energies must commence for us to feel fully whole and complete. When these two energies harmonize, we thrive.

When the sacred feminine aspects of surrender, creativity, intuition, and vulnerability coincide with the sacred masculine aspects of responsibility, proactiveness, and strength, we experience true empowerment. Anything that comes our way can be handled with both grace and courage because we are complete within, and we trust ourselves to make wise decisions and choose aligned actions.

JULY 27

Honor and nourish your womb. Your womb is a portal between worlds; it is where all your creations are conceived and cared for. It is the source of your creativity, your ability to connect with others, and your feminine power.

Care for your womb by being mindful of the food and drink you put into your body, the feminine products you use, and the people you allow entrance to it. Honor your womb by utilizing your power, trusting your intuition, and allowing creative energy to flow through you.

JULY 28

The magic of life is present in all things, always. There are moments in your journey that are very big and assume dominance over the smaller, seemingly insignificant moments. Let yourself be thrilled with each huge milestone, but also remember to be grateful for those in-between days. The periods of time separating milestones are just as important as, if not more important than, the big events. These days are the culmination of those unforgettable occurrences. To forget the pain, tears, love, and hard work put into the manifestation of those milestones is a sin. Always remember where you came from and how much effort you put into getting where you are. And when things slow down again, be present. Life is happening every day, and you don't want to miss it by projecting your consciousness into the next fleeting milestone.

JULY 29

Love is the root of all soul connections. This can be hard to see and accept sometimes because when you have been mistreated, you tend to only remember the pain caused by the other person or the hurt you felt when they walked out of your life. On a soul level, you both love each other. If you did not, you would not have come together in this lifetime. To heal from heartaches, it's important to view your relationships through the eyes of your higher self. Even though you felt broken by a relationship, you would not be who you are if you did not experience it. You do not need to forgive if you are not ready, and you are right to cut off access to your energy when someone is not meeting you on your level. But to break down the walls that have risen around your heart, and to allow softness into your heart again, you must accept what has happened and how it has changed you. Then you will be free.

JULY 30

Being committed to yourself and your rising requires you to make the decision to never abandon or undermine yourself again. Too often you may hold yourself captive by silencing your truth to keep others comfortable. Perhaps you refrain from saying what needs to be said in favor of avoiding conflict and "keeping the peace." By doing this, you only hurt yourself, and you are far from feeling at peace. It's better to address what needs addressing than sacrifice your well-being for a façade.

Forgive yourself for times when you undermined yourself. Let the goddess within rise and wash away all behaviors that no longer serve you. Embody your strength, and affirm that you have your back from now on.

JULY 31

Part of the reason we are on this planet in these bodies is to learn how to use our souls' gifts. We have the ability to tune in to different frequencies to understand how they work and what may happen if we follow a certain path. We have the ability to communicate telepathically, connect with spirits, and draw forth information that is unknown to our other senses. We can manifest our dreams and align with our highest timelines. We are enrolled in this Earth school to unlock these abilities and use them to jump into a higher timeline as a collective. This timeline is rooted in love and compassion for the self, others, and Mother Earth. As we rise into our full potential, and accept and hone our abilities, a new world will be born.

AUGUST 1

Lammas, also known as Lughnasadh in Irish traditions, is the first of three harvest festivals on the Celtic Wheel of the Year. It is the midway point between the summer solstice and the fall equinox; it is still summer, but the telltale signs of autumn are starting to appear, shifting the collective energy.

The omnipresent Goddess is still in her Mother energy and is birthing abundance for all her children. The omnipresent God is growing older and preparing for his final days in his current incarnation. The pace of things is starting to slow as the excitement of summer winds down and mental preparation for the winter months

Lammas is a time for practicing gratitude, utilizing our talents, and taking in our first harvests.

AUGUST 2

Your relationships with people and things outside yourself are meant to enrich your life, not take away from it. If you continue to entertain relationships or habits that you know have run their course, you will feel depleted, burned out, or simply disappointed.

Instead of putting the blame on the other person or situation, go within yourself. You are the one who will have to make a change if you want to feel enriched, not drained. You will know when the time is right for you to move on. Bless what you're leaving behind with love, and make the best decision for your health and well-being.

AUGUST 3

Dwelling on your regrets keeps you locked in stagnation. Choosing to let your past go and improve yourself is one of the best decisions you will ever make. Self-forgiveness is a courageous act of unconditional love.

You have the power to change at any time, and you have the sacred ability to transmute pain into growth. Weed through your experiences and hold on to the lessons learned, releasing any embarrassment, guilt, or regret lingering there. It is up to you to take accountability and define yourself through your values in the present, not your mistakes of the past. It doesn't matter what you feel you did wrong previously; what matters is that you apply the wisdom gained from these moments and make different choices moving forward. Direct your attention toward how you want to feel now.

AUGUST 4

Collectively, human consciousness is changing, all over the planet. Everyone is evolving and vibrations are rising. Ancient wisdom of the Divine Feminine is swirling all around you, encompassing you in love, light, and high vibrations. As you embrace this powerful energy, you begin to embody it.

If you feel you are changing as the world changes, but you aren't sure how to feel about it all, don't worry. Your innate power is nothing to be afraid of. It is safe for you to be powerful; you are *destined* to be powerful. It is okay for you to reinvent yourself. You are an ever-expanding, ever-evolving Divine Feminine.

AUGUST 5

Filling yourself with love first transforms your entire life. Your relationships improve, your work gets better, and the quality of your life in general is enhanced.

Through self-love you realize everything is connected, and you no longer feel the need to prove yourself, claim another, or align yourself to anything other than your own heart. You see all relationships and experiences as moments in your journey to hold dear, yet you remain unattached to them. You can enjoy your present with gratitude because you are not worried about clutching onto a person, place, or thing forever. You know the only constant in your life is your inner relationship with yourself; therefore, every fleeting moment can be thoroughly cherished.

AUGUST 6

You do not have to do anything that doesn't feel aligned to you. Part of your purpose is to forge a path that is authentic to you, no matter how it differs from the paths of your peers. You will never *get it wrong* when you act on the guidance of your soul. Listen to what your higher mind is sharing with you; follow the whispers of your heart. Release self-sabotaging mindsets that say you are not good enough for the dreams you have. You are exactly the right person to live the visions you've seen in your mind's eye. If it wasn't meant for you, you wouldn't feel called to it.

AUGUST 7

Spiritual union between an aligned Divine Feminine and an aligned Divine Masculine is the energy the planet needs now. A Divine Feminine deserves a Divine Masculine counterpart, and a Divine Masculine deserves a Divine Feminine. You deserve someone who sees and honors the goddess that you are. If you are entertaining partners who don't fully see you, focus on self-love. The more you empower and love yourself, the more in tune with your Divine Feminine energy you are. When you're aligned with your Divine Feminine energy, you create space for a true Divine Masculine to enter your experience. When these two energies collide, society changes. Your love creates worlds.

AUGUST 8

The Goddess comes in many different forms. From the understanding and compassionate Kuan Yin to the fierce and destructive Kali Ma, the Goddess has many faces and embodiments. She is the destroyer when circumstances must end, and the mother when nurturing is required. In each of her forms, no matter how light or dark, she moves in the name of love. Let her image be a reminder to you that every color of yourself serves a purpose. Your anger, your joy, your sadness, and your bliss are all real and beautiful. Your many faces are an expression of the Goddess, and they all contribute to the evolution of your being. Let every side of you be seen, be heard. For there is nothing more inspiring than a person who knows their worth and loves themselves enough to express the many voices of their soul.

AUGUST 9

Some days it's hard to get out of bed. Sometimes you just want to go to sleep and stay there for months. And that's okay.

What matters is that you are showing up for yourself. Showing up for you doesn't always mean getting out in the world and expressing yourself. Sometimes showing up for you can mean honoring your body's cry for rest or your mind's demand for sleep. Showing up for you also looks like knowing when it is time to get things done and knowing when it is time to move beyond your comfort zone.

The key is to create balance between these two extremes. Make time for being productive, and make time regularly for rest and renewal. Connect with your body; learn its rhythms and cycles. When you feel your scales dipping too far to one side, do something to shift the energy. Practice moderation in all things, and know that it is okay to be still. You don't have to be on all the time. Restore, so when you do turn back on, you do so with full power.

AUGUST 10

We need to stop looking at other women as enemies. We must honor our differences and stop allowing them to separate us. Remember, the patriarchy wants us to stay divided because it is intimidated by the idea of strong women coming together. No matter what, we must love our sisters and fight for them. When women come together, love each other, and lift each other up, we will see incredible shifts in society.

AUGUST 11

You are not next to godliness, for you are an expression of the Divine. You are a goddess and it is your divine birthright to feel the pleasures that come with being one. Denying yourself pleasure is an insult to the Divine.

Make it a point to activate your inner Venus. Seek pleasure each day, especially among the mundane. Go on a quest to find life's sweetest fruit, and let her juices run down your chin as you sink your teeth into your present moment in surrender to divine ecstasy. Cultivate pleasure in your environment, through all your senses and within the company you keep. Look for the beauty in all things and experiences, and never stop searching for the best life has to offer. You are here to bite into life and savor her nectar. You are meant to experience pleasure beyond your greatest fantasy.

AUGUST 12

Truth is a familiar friend, and when it comes back around, you feel comforted, joyful, and solid. As your path unfolds, you will experience many twists and turns, people and opportunities, opinions and facts. Depending on the company you keep or the environments you find yourself in, your thoughts and mind will change many times. Throughout it all, your truth remains the same. Each time you stray from your truth, it will reel you back in. Clarity will wash over your vessel as you soak in the bliss of returning home again.

AUGUST 13

Your body is the conduit between the ethereal and the physical planes. It senses things your logical mind may not initially pick up. It tells you when your aura is being clouded and shows you where your energy is draining. As a result, your body is always fluctuating. It feels better to be in your body on some days and worse on others. When dealing with illness, or experiencing aches and pains, work with your body, not against it, to manifest health and wellness. Your body is wise, and it is only trying to help your emotional and spiritual bodies align. Honor the way you feel every day. Nourish your body with healthy foods, herbs, and plenty of rest. Learn the way your body works, and tend to its cycles for optimum well-being.

AUGUST 14

At the time of the full moon, you may feel more intuitive or more whole, or find that situations that were previously troubling you have become easier to understand. The light of the full moon illuminates all that was previously hidden from you. Manifestations set with the last new moon are waxing, and you are gaining clarity. Use this time to check in with yourself and your goals. Decide if your current trajectory is working for you or if you need to make adjustments. Listen to your inner wisdom, find gratitude for all that's manifested for you, and enjoy time with your loved ones. This is a time of completion and celebration.

AUGUST 15

You will never know whether you will succeed if you don't try. You can dream very big, but sometimes you may refrain from pursuing your dreams because you are overwhelmed by all you would have to tackle to make those dreams a reality. To raise your confidence levels in yourself, your dreams, and the Universe, set a small goal for yourself, one that can be achieved easily, and make it happen. Do this as much as you feel guided to, and embrace the sense of accomplishment that comes with each task you complete. This will show you that what you desire *can* and *will* come to fruition, no matter the size of the manifestation.

AUGUST 16

Divinity is not something you become; it is something you *are*. You are born of the stars to live freely in the physical realm, exploring the mysteries of human life and how this experience intertwines with All That Is. You are a divine being, expressing your true essence through the love you cultivate and share with others. To fulfill your purpose is to be authentic in your nature. Sovereignty takes precedence when you accept all that you are and let nothing stand in the way of your divine beingness.

AUGUST 17

Any relationship that crumbles because of your being your authentic self was not a solid relationship to begin with. If a house's foundation is rotted, you can't expect it to remain standing. Sure, you can tiptoe around being careful not to step in a space where the floor could fall through, but do you really want to live your life that way?

You deserve a strong foundation to build from. Liberate yourself and don't look back. You aren't missing anything—something much better and far more aligned to you is on its way.

AUGUST 18

What you see on social media, in magazines, or on television is not real life. All media is an expression of someone else's soul. Whether that expression stems from negative or positive energy is only known by the soul who created it. And that is why comparing yourself and your life to what you see in the media is extremely harmful.

You can never really know what another being is experiencing within themselves. Jealousy, comparison, and judgment only lower your vibration and cloud your perception of your own life. If you see something in the media that stirs these feelings within you, sit with it. Think about why that is and what you can do about it. Let the feelings social media stirs within you empower your self-exploration practices, not take away from your own experience.

AUGUST 19

There are no rules. The Earth is an ongoing dream of the Divine. In this space, you can do whatever you want. You have been granted with free will. No one can tell you who you are or what you should be doing. No one can exert their will over yours. Think consciously about who your heart is guiding you to be. Discover the goddess dwelling within you and let her take the wheel. You are the creatrix in your life. Own this title and unleash her full force.

AUGUST 20

The greatest act of service you can provide is shining your inner light. You are most beautiful when you show up as your authentic self and let others into your heart. It's your willingness to be real and raw that empowers others to shed their own masks and be free. It's the love you hold for yourself that helps others love themselves. As you fearlessly live your truth, you illuminate the truths of others.

Your divine duty is to rise in your power and lead through your heart-based example. Radiating your truth and confidently sharing your essence with the world is what brings positive change to the world. As you rise into your full potential, an energetic ripple effect arises and spreads throughout the collective, activating the masses and helping them rise in their own way. As people everywhere learn to be and love themselves, a new, better way of being is born.

AUGUST 21

Grow your circle of friends and acquaintances so you can accrue greater universal wisdom. Everyone you meet, no matter how like-minded, comes from a different walk of life from yours. It is through your connections with others that you begin to see the world from fresh perspectives. You may be a master of your craft, yet someone may come along who shows you a new way of doing things. It is your willingness to learn and be open with others that will not only enrich your human experience but will also complement your soul's evolution.

AUGUST 22

You have the power. You have the power to remove yourself from one-sided relationships. You have the power to say what you really mean and say it with love. You have the strength to pick yourself back up again after heartbreak. You have the courage to face yourself, and so you have the courage to face the world.

Your power is always within you. There is never a time when you cannot access it. Trust yourself enough to know that when the time comes, you will extend the full force of your power to overcome every obstacle on your path.

AUGUST 23

Build upon the connection you have with all things. Bless and pray over your food and water. Infuse everything you consume with the pure white light of the Divine through visualization. Cleanse new items brought into your home, especially things that will be in your sacred space. Your will and divine energy can be used to influence everything in your life, no matter how average something may seem. Direct your energy where you want it to go. Weave your soul into everything you do, and you will see proof that magic exists.

AUGUST 24

We put so much focus on the negative things people say and do that we overlook the kind things they say and do. When someone gives us a compliment or expresses their love and support, we need to welcome their offerings with open arms. Abundance comes in many forms, one of which is through the kindness of others.

We tend to push people away or shrug off their loving gestures if we have given our trust before, only to see it broken. Denying another's genuine offerings shows the Universe we feel we do not deserve positive interactions in our experience moving forward. This all comes down to our level of self-worth. When we feel unworthy, it is difficult for us to receive the kindness of another's heart.

It's time to stop assuming the worst of people and the worst for ourselves, and start seeing the good in everyone. As we work on our self-worth, choosing to recognize the good in us, we will naturally see more good in others and be able to share our positive energy free from inhibitions. We can change the narrative. We are worthy of pleasant interactions and trustworthy relationships, and it is safe for us to have these.

AUGUST 25

Celebrate you. You deserve every good thing that comes your way. You are allowed to jump up and down, and cry, and laugh as you witness your manifestations coming to fruition. Ride the wave of exhilaration that comes when you attract what you desire and get to finally experience it. Soak up this energy; cherish it and love it. You have put so much work into yourself and into your life to get where you are today. Draw in all the positive energy and hold it close to your heart. You have done incredible things, and you aren't finished yet. Let yourself revel in the joy of a job well done.

AUGUST 26

Showing up as your authentic self takes courage. Speaking a truth you've held within for ages can spark a reaction in your body. Taking action toward a long-awaited dream creates a response within your chakras. As you step more fully into all that you are, show up as your authentic self, and speak your truth, your aura and body are cleared of blocks that previously held you back. This may create a few moments of discomfort, but there comes a time when you must ask yourself what is worse: momentarily feeling discomfort as you claim your truth, or living a lifetime of uneasiness while ignoring your truth? Dig within and pull out the strength lying in there. Give your authenticity full rein, and speak what's in your heart. Stand by your truth and you will always be pleased with the results that follow.

AUGUST 27

Difficulties in love oftentimes come from programming that is active within you. If you hold negative beliefs about men, for example, you will continue to attract men who display those traits. If you think women have to behave in a certain way to attract and keep a man, you will try to contain yourself in some mold that is inauthentic to you, only to end up being rejected by the partner you were trying so hard to hold on to.

You have to be willing to go within and change your core beliefs about the people you are attracted to (of any sex or sexual orientation), and your core beliefs about yourself, if you really want to have a successful romantic partnership in your life. Assuming all men disrespect women sends a signal to the Universe that you are looking for more men who are disrespectful to women. Assuming no one loves you tells the Universe you want to continue feeling unloved.

Examine your deepest beliefs about yourself and your potential partners. Reprogram yourself by aligning your core beliefs with love. If you want love, you've got to be in the love vibration.

AUGUST 28

It's not about the things you do; it's about how good you feel while doing them. When your soul puts up resistance to things that are not in alignment with who you are at your core, your inner peace suffers.

Your essence craves a certain kind of stimulation, and that is something only you can define. Success, like beauty, is in the eye of the beholder. What fulfills you will vary from what fulfills your peers. It is your responsibility to go within and discover the things that light you up. Life is too short to spend time doing things that don't feel right to you. Find the things that do, and make attracting them your sole purpose.

AUGUST 29

Every day provides you with the opportunity to start, or start again. Time is an illusion, but what's real is your ability to create through love. There is no need to race against the calendar or wait for your birthday to start anew. You have the power within to make waves every single day. Don't wait. Life is happening now. Take heed of the stirrings deep within your vessel. Move with the ferocity of the Dark Goddess, and don't take no for an answer. You do not have to settle; you do not have to bide your time. Trust that your inner guidance will always help you make the best decisions for you, and once you know what you need to do, don't delay. There will never come a time when you will feel 100 percent ready. Take life by the reins and embark on your journey today.

AUGUST 30

Just because it hurts to say good-bye doesn't mean a relationship is meant to stay in your life. At some point you must do what is best for you and the course your life is taking. If a friendship or romantic partnership is having a negative impact on you and your goals despite your putting in the work to heal the relationship, it's best to walk away, no matter how much love was shared between you.

In these times, know it is okay to grieve. You are allowed to cry for what is gone and honor the end of an era. Let yourself feel all that you are feeling, with the knowing that the sun will rise again, and you will be blessed with many new relationships that will undeniably support your evolution.

AUGUST 31

The Mother has brought you her medicine, and you have embraced wholeness within. Your heart is full of love for yourself and all the beautiful people in your life. You understand your power and know how to utilize it in the healthiest ways. You are blessed with many loving and balanced relationships, and you are being showered with wonderful opportunities for continued growth. You are whole; you are complete. You can handle whatever comes your way because you are your greatest friend and partner. Your creativity is overflowing, and you use it to bring your manifestations to life. You see beauty and abundance everywhere you look. You proudly take up space as a goddess of Earth and the cosmos.

PART THREE

THE CRONE

*"In the infinity of life where I am,
all is perfect, whole, and complete.
I no longer choose to believe in old limitations
and lack. I now choose to begin to see myself
as the Universe sees me—perfect,
whole, and complete."*

— Louise Hay, *You Can Heal Your Life*

SEPTEMBER 1

The third aspect of the Divine Feminine is the Crone. She is our inner sage, ruling our intuition, shadow, and universal wisdom. She reigns over the late fall and winter months, the waning moon, and the dark of night. Traditionally she is linked with the end of a woman's life; however, our Crone is activated whenever we draw our energy inward in search of answers and solitude. Our Crone guides us through life transitions, protects us as we release what no longer serves, and cradles us when we experience loss.

The Crone is not weak; she is the almighty Dark Goddess, and she grants us the ability to set boundaries, move in favor of our worth, and transmute fear and rage into love and dynamic action.

Crone energy may seem looming at first, but it is a part of who we are. If we let her draw our awareness to what has died in our lives, she can carry us through the threshold of liberation and rebirth.

SEPTEMBER 2

The Divine Feminine is present within everything; she is active and alive in all religious figures, belief systems, and spiritual practices as well. It is the feminine energy within everyone that creates all things. Without feminine energy, nothing would ever be conceived or born.

With this knowledge, know you do not have to follow any one religion or spiritual practice. You have the right to explore any belief system that calls to you, while still connecting with the Divine Feminine. There truly are no "rules" when it comes to connecting with the Divine.

Craft your own practices, your own beliefs. Borrow from any religion or belief system you feel called to. Take what feels right to you and let the rest go. Know that if a spiritual belief you once held no longer resonates, that is okay too. You are allowed to evolve. You are a spiritual being by nature, and your soul knows what rings true for you and which beliefs will best guide you in different parts of your journey.

SEPTEMBER 3

Just as you contain both feminine and masculine energy within, you also hold dark and light polarities. Your shadow is the part of you that holds your darker energy. Where lighter energy is focused more on positive aspects such as love or harmony, your shadow side holds more negative aspects, such as fear or jealousy.

Your shadow self is far from *bad*, however, and it certainly does not mean you any harm. There is no reason to feel ashamed about the darker aspects of yourself. Learning to embrace your shadow is a major part of knowing and loving yourself. Embracing your shadow does not mean that you will become an alternative, darker version of you, but rather that you acknowledge those aspects of yourself. Instead of fighting to suppress these aspects, accept them, knowing they are part of what makes you who you are; and no matter what darkness dwells inside, you are worthy of the things you desire.

SEPTEMBER 4

Discerning between intuition and fear can be very simple. Intuition comes through subtly and calmly. Fear comes through frantically and chaotically.

Your intuition will never be too excited in either direction, positive or negative. It will always speak to you in a calm manner, telling you what you need to know, and nothing more. Fear comes through loudly, in an intimidating way. Fear tells you stories that scare you and keep you blocked. Your intuition will never tell you anything of the sort. Even if your intuition is bringing you a warning, it will not be exaggerated. Pay attention to the vibration you *feel*, and you will soon be able to discern between the two.

SEPTEMBER 5

Part of the fun of living on planet Earth is experiencing contrast. You are here to enjoy your life in ways only you can.

If something displeases you, let it go, and find something that is more pleasing. If something doesn't work for you but works for someone else, let them have their fun. If something works for you but not those around you, keep having your fun. You have your own delightful experiences to explore. You are not here to please and be pleased. You are not here to be a copy of another. You don't have to agree with others about everything all the time. Let the contrast exhilarate you.

SEPTEMBER 6

None of your emotions is innately *bad*; emotions are simply another expression of your energy. You may prefer feeling happy and content to feeling sad and uncomfortable, but just because you prefer feeling good does not mean there is no value in feeling bad.

The patriarchal society teaches that even in times of strife, you should continue your life as normal. To a certain extent, continuing your regular routine can be healthy. But if you completely ignore your emotions during a very negative period in your life, stuffing your feelings down and continuing as normal, you do yourself a massive disservice.

Ignoring your emotions is a surefire way to create an imbalance within your mind, body, and spirit. If you stop and allow your "bad" feelings a chance to express themselves, you may find that they exit your vibration much faster than if you continue to silence them. Be mindful of your feelings' feelings and find healthy ways to express them. Learn what you can from lower emotions, and honor yourself where you are.

SEPTEMBER 7

Clarity comes when it is time for it to come. Sometimes a situation in your life will be confusing, and purposely so. There is a reason for everything you experience; it does not matter what it is or how it occurs. There is a reason for it being in your life.

You are not meant to know the reason why things happen right when you want to know it. Life is a mystery, and it is one that you can enjoy solving, or else why would you return? Let the mystery of life unfold for you; refrain from squeezing answers out of everything. Sit back, seek peace, and let the answers to your questions come through when the time is right. Clarity always comes, just not usually on your watch. Trust the process.

SEPTEMBER 8

Holding expectations is only a problem when you are trying to manipulate situations. When you attempt to manipulate, you are focused on the lack of something, not the presence of what you desire. In truth, the Divine knows what is best for you. Feeling the urge to manipulate is a sign you need to shift into surrender.

Try not to focus on things that are outside your control. Instead, hold high expectations for yourself. Expect good health, lots of love, abundance, and prosperity, and trust that the Divine will continue to bless you with these things. Hold positive expectations without attempting to control situations, and you will see positive results.

SEPTEMBER 9

Letting go of past hurts and disappointments is a necessary part of healing. It is one we may meet with a lot of resistance; we fear releasing our pain for many different reasons. Sometimes we may fear forgetting the love that was present before the pain arrived. Other times we may fear the unknown, as we are accustomed to living with this heartache and it has become comfortable. The way we can free ourselves is by changing the narrative.

Instead of looking at something that played out in our past as a hindrance and repeating the same old movie in our minds, let's shift our perspective. Let's look for ways in which our past experiences helped mold us into the people we are today. Let's replace negative thoughts about what happened with positive thoughts about the wisdom and growth we walked away with. Changing the narrative creates space in our minds and bodies for the healing to take place.

SEPTEMBER 10

The Universe and spirit world communicate in a lot of different ways. You may hear repeated words or phrases, see repetitive number sequences, or receive signs in the form of feathers, coins, or other things that have significance to you. Sometimes you may feel frustrated as you keep seeing or hearing the signs that your manifestations are on the way, but you have yet to see any "real proof" in the physical world.

Repeated signs and synchronicities are confirmation that your manifestations are coming to life. Instead of getting angry at the repetitive messages you are seeing—or worse, angry at the Universe—welcome them with an open heart and show your appreciation. If you weren't meant to experience this manifestation at some point in your life journey, you wouldn't be receiving the signs pointing to yes in the first place.

SEPTEMBER 11

My grandmother taught me that life moves in circles. She told me the longer we live, the more we will see old patterns come back around again. I believe this happens for a few reasons. One is that there is a cycle engrained in our vibration that life is trying to draw our attention to so we can overcome it. The other is that we are not always ready for certain people and opportunities when they initially show up—we need more time to evolve so the situation can really work for us.

The best thing for us to do is to keep working on ourselves; keep living our lives. Everything that is meant for us comes in divine timing. Improving ourselves and inviting joy into our days helps us align with our highest good. In this space, we are a magnet for the blessings that belong to us.

SEPTEMBER 12

As the energy of our planet changes, people everywhere are experiencing spiritual awakenings and delving deeper into their spiritual practices. Many in the spiritual community talk about personal ascension and enlightenment—as the energy of the planet rises, our consciousness is also expanding. The consciousness of the Universe and the consciousness of humanity are playing off each other, bringing about the great shift in Divine Feminine energy and the balancing of energy between Divine Feminine and Divine Masculine. This is certainly something to be celebrated.

However, we cannot let our personal ascension interfere with our human experience. We cannot use enlightenment to avoid feeling. We cannot use our awakening as an excuse to ignore our responsibilities. If we do, we will only fall backward into the toxic patriarchal ways of being once more. Spirituality is not an escape; it is a supplement to everything we are.

SEPTEMBER 13

It is your nature to want to know everything about how your life will turn out. You may look outside yourself seeking answers about who you are, where you are going, and how you will get there.

The moment you stop looking outside yourself is the moment you find peace. Turn inward and connect with the Divine. Constantly seeking answers from outside yourself sends out the vibration that you are not satisfied with your current life. And when you make this your prominent vibration, you will repeatedly feel dissatisfaction with where you are.

Choose to stop chasing the next best thing. Instead, bring your awareness to where you are in this moment. Remember that where you currently stand is somewhere you once desperately wanted to be. Give thanks for what you have, while also allowing your dreams for the future to become clear. Trust that every answer you are seeking lies within you. And when the time is right, everything you want will align perfectly for you.

SEPTEMBER 14

Love every part of yourself that isn't the prettiest. Love your darkness as you love your light. Find gratitude for your wrongdoings and forgive yourself for your mistakes. Accept the role you have played at different stages of your life. Everything you have ever done or experienced has made you the person you are today. The past cannot be rewritten, but the future is a blank page. Know that you have power over the habits, traits, and beliefs that you want to change. All you must do is love yourself a little more and trust yourself to make the best decisions for you moving forward, based on the wisdom you have previously acquired. When you are gentle with yourself, your toxic patterns can and will be redirected.

SEPTEMBER 15

From the full moon to the new moon, the moon is waning, and your feminine energy is waning too. The dark moon happens in the days just before a new moon, when the moon has waned completely and no light can be seen from it. This part of the moon cycle is connected to the feminine archetype of the Crone and her magical ability to release. The last moon cycle is ending, and a new one is about to begin—outdated energy is making its exit under the influence of the Crone and is preparing to be reborn as the Maiden when the new moon occurs.

Use this time to cleanse your mind, body, and soul. If there is anything in your life, whether it be something external or internal, that you are ready to be rid of, the two weeks between the full moon and the new moon are the perfect time to focus on letting go and moving on. When the new moon comes, focus on the new energy you want to invite into your experience.

SEPTEMBER 16

Too often we withhold our true emotions for made-up reasons in our minds. Sometimes we may say we don't want to express our true feelings for the sake of another. Sometimes we may say we "can't" experience a certain emotion for fear of how others may perceive us. We also make up rules like "I'm spiritual, so I can't be angry" or "I'm logical, so I can't be frustrated over something silly like this."

By affirming statements like these, we are telling our body and soul that it is wrong to feel and that our feelings are invalid. This only goes on to create an even greater state of disharmony within. Resentment and hatred are born of denying our worth.

Sometimes it can feel like a challenge to communicate our full truth to ourselves and others, but if we don't, we will continue to feel unworthy until our desires and needs are expressed.

SEPTEMBER 17

Death is oftentimes labeled taboo, but it is inevitable. You are eventually going to transition from this plane, and although this can be terrifying to the ego, it is accepted by your soul. You can learn a lot about yourself and your true desires by pondering the concept of your own death.

When you're comfortable, consider the end of your life in a gentle and observational way. Put yourself in the time and space of your body before exiting your current experience. How does she feel as her life ends? What did she accomplish? More importantly, what did she *feel*? Did she love? Did she cry? Did she dare to challenge the norm and forge her own path? Did she say yes only when she meant it and no only when she meant it? In this reflective projection, how fulfilled are you? What comes up as you ponder the end of your experience as this person, in this body, in this part of history? Start there.

SEPTEMBER 18

Spirituality is the language of life; the two are synonymous. Neither one can exist without the other. We are all created from the same Source energy, no matter our individual spiritual or religious paths. And so, spirituality is intricately intertwined with all life. There are correlating patterns between various religions, and similar teachings from philosophers and spiritualists, for this reason. There is one constant in all living beings and that is Source energy. Life is designed to help us reconnect with our Source energy, and Source energy is our guidance through life.

SEPTEMBER 19

Your silence is part of your allure. In your silence, you connect with your inner voice and find clarity. Not everything deserves a response from you. Withdrawing your energy from the outside world fuels your spirit and brings answers; retreating inward is an act of power that brings healing and understanding. Everything you need is within you—you must only go within and discover what is hidden there.

If there are people in your life who don't see your worth, limit their access to you. Let yourself be led by your inner voice. Take up space and be big about it. Move in silence, ensuring that what you hold sacred stays that way. When you are ready for your reveal, the world will follow suit.

SEPTEMBER 20

Mabon is the second harvest festival on the Celtic Wheel of the Year. The seasons are shifting, and it is clear that summer has ended and Earth's colors and liveliness are beginning to fade away. Mabon aligns with the autumn equinox; there is equal balance between daylight and nighttime hours on Mabon. Following this day, the sun is preparing for its departure into the darkness of winter.

This is a time to be grateful for all your manifestations that bore fruit during the year, whether they were something in your external world or something that came to be within you.

To honor the season, connect with loved ones and express your deepest appreciation for their companionship. Utilize this time to take stock in your own life. What have you accomplished this year that you set out to do at the beginning of the year? How have your plans changed? What do you still need to mark off your list before the end of the year?

SEPTEMBER 21

Everything about you is beautiful, and it is you who must see and believe this in order to fully embrace your power. Beauty goes far beyond physical looks and appearance. Beauty comes from within you, and it encompasses both your light and dark aspects. You do not need to try to be anything that you are not. You do not need to pretend or force yourself to fit into a space that you know is not for you. Your beauty comes alive when you accept all that you are and forge your own path forward. It does not matter who you used to be, or what you feel you did by mistake. You are beautiful no matter what you have done, no matter what has been done to you. You were beautiful before these things happened, while they happened, and even now as they are in the past. See yourself for the beauty that you are and welcome healing into your heart.

SEPTEMBER 22

Art and literature are the real time capsules, and as such, should be held sacred. History portrayed through someone else's lens helps you understand where you came from and gives a broader perspective regarding where you are going. Anything you need can be found through creative expression of the past. Expressions of love, feelings of hope, someone singing the blues: these are the stories that can shape you. And with each, an esoteric companionship to another soul in another time is developed.

Art, music, and literature deserve your protection. Human expression is what keeps you going. Tune in to your Divine Feminine energy by engaging in creative outlets. Allow your soul to express itself.

SEPTEMBER 23

We dream life in movie montages, forgetting there is a real process to all things. We get upset when our desires don't manifest overnight. We lose hope when we don't see physical proof that our circumstances are changing.

The Divine Feminine is asking us to slow down. Movies skip the drawn-out periods of time when it seems like nothing is moving forward and nothing ever will. Films primarily focus on the parts of the story deemed worthy of being shown, but there's a lot happening during the scenes that aren't written. We can find comfort in knowing that the illusion of stagnation is what makes the result much more gratifying. We're the real characters in the movie that is life. If there is one thing we can take from film, it's that our time always comes. Let's be patient and allow ourselves to enjoy the in-between scenes.

SEPTEMBER 24

Your darker emotions deserve to be heard just as much as your lighter ones do. It's not that you should always act upon what your darker emotions are relaying to you—acting from a place of darkness will only invite more darkness into your life. Remember, like attracts like.

But to acknowledge and work through your darker emotions, that's where the treasure is. Let yourself feel low. Negating your emotions using spirituality as your comfort blanket does not equal true healing. Heal yourself by exploring your own darkness. Peel back your layers and get to the root cause of your bad mood. Burn away what's clouding your judgment, and really strive to understand yourself. Then rise from the ashes, transformed and reborn.

SEPTEMBER 25

The goddess within ages with grace, and she never stops expanding. With each passing year, recognize how you have become more and more beautiful, both inside and out. Your body is a sacred and intimate diary. It travels with you throughout your life and holds the memories of all you've experienced. As you gaze upon your body, reflect upon the different versions of you that you've known, and send each of them love. Embrace your evolution; open your arms to even more new and improved versions of yourself.

Keep your mind fresh. Learn, ask questions, and be willing to broaden your perspective. Seek the thrill of discovering more about those around you and more about yourself. Dive deep within yourself; continue to try to understand yourself better. Let your guard down and be vulnerable with others. Open your heart and accept new challenges with faith. Say yes to life and be in harmony with it. Set the intention to enjoy your later years just as much as you did your earlier ones, and maybe even a little more. Allow life to keep getting better and better.

SEPTEMBER 26

The purpose of a good meditation session is to align your energy, mind, body, and soul. There is no way you can meditate incorrectly; your meditation practice is just as unique as your soul. Don't force it to be a certain way, and release any expectations you have. Design your meditation practice in a way that feels right to you. You may enjoy lying down with New Age music playing in the background, or you may find walking in nature is your preferred way to meditate. Meditation is best used to replenish your essence, so you must choose a meditation practice that really feeds your inner being. When you find it, use your practice to discover your inner sanctum. Tune in to silence and revitalize your senses. Be open to the sensations and insights that come to you; detach from the thoughts entering your mind. Let your spirit take you on a journey, and simply observe. Wisdom comes when you are silently submerged in your own energy.

SEPTEMBER 27

A wise woman is confident in herself. She knows who she is; she knows her own heart. She understands what drives her and what her core values are. A woman who is confident in who she is doesn't feel the need to judge another. She sees that each person on this planet has their own path to walk, and everyone is living in the most perfect way for themselves.

A wise woman's duty is not to manipulate the decisions of her children, loved ones, peers, or others. A wise woman offers guidance and support when needed, and never tries to sway someone one way or another. Through her influence, a wise woman can inspire the masses just by giving them the space to be themselves and explore the endless paths before them.

SEPTEMBER 28

There is a great difference between what you feel you *should do* and what you *must do*. The word *should* provides the connotation that what you're being made to do is beyond your control. The word *must* presents the idea that what you're doing is something you feel absolutely guided to do.

Divine Feminine energy is always flowing; such is the way of the Goddess. To give your feminine energy full rein, surrender to the motion of flowing. When you feel guided to do something—when there is something you *must* do—do it as long as you feel you must. Because feminine energy flows, it is always changing and evolving. If what was once a must turns into a should, let yourself flow on from it, as it is no longer in alignment with the goddess you are.

SEPTEMBER 29

Shifting from your Mother aspect to your Crone aspect stirs feelings of emptiness where there was once a space brimming with abundance. Whether this shift is related to the ending of a situation or a relationship, whether it is related to physical changes in your body, or whether you are experiencing a loss of another kind, it can feel frightening to let go of what once was. This space is not only about loss or what is gone, however. This space is also about what you have gained in terms of wisdom and experience. Find peace in this shift, in whatever way you are undergoing it. If you did not experience that fullness, you would never know how blessed you are to live this human life. If you did not experience any endings, you would never have welcomed in all the love and light you have lived. Accept what is over, and rejoice in what has been. You've seen well by now that everything that leaves your life is replaced by something even greater.

SEPTEMBER 30

Resonance is a facet of intuition. Just as you may intuitively *know* something, you will also just *know* when something resonates with you. When two energies that complement each other combine, the mind, body, and soul all feel this. This can happen with another person, with a message, with a song, a location, an animal—anything. To resonate with something or someone is to be touched by the soul of that being. You will not be able to deny that your energy opened to receive this other energy because your entire being will feel it. And when something comes through that strong, that's how you know it is for you.

OCTOBER 1

Your soul is a vast ocean, expanding endlessly in every direction. There is so much beauty and magic dwelling within your vessel that you can't even begin to appreciate all that you are in one sitting. Make discovering yourself an ongoing sacred practice in your life. As the wheel turns, you grow and evolve, unlocking more of the treasure that is you, and you release old identities and ways of being that you no longer need carry. With each new age, you learn more about who you really are. Never fear getting older. Rejoice in the knowing that with each new year, you will once again experience the pleasure of getting to know you.

OCTOBER 2

Some things simply don't deserve your energy. You do not have to be available to everyone all the time. You do not have to continue previously made agreements if they are not working for you anymore. Activate your inner Dark Goddess when you need space to work through your own emotions. Retreat into your inner world and when you are in the right space to respond, reemerge. Utilize her power to set boundaries and protect yourself. Let her express your true emotions to the people in your life. Even though it can be uncomfortable sometimes, you must let others know when they are overstepping your boundaries or hurting your feelings.

Use discernment every day, no matter where you go or who you rendezvous with. Pay attention to how certain environments or company affect your energy, and honor yourself by removing yourself from energies that don't feel right anymore. You are allowed to move differently; in fact, your rising requires you to do so.

You are not meant to sacrifice your power and your growth for others. With your vibration, make it clear that if you are not being respected, others only have two options: rise along with you or get left behind.

OCTOBER 3

For speaking her truth and being loud about it, a woman can be condemned under the patriarchy. Since the beginning of time, men have taken strong women and demonized, sexualized, and patronized them. If a woman dares speak out, she is punished or made to look insane.

Lilith, the first woman and most likely the first feminist, was created with Adam, from the same soil. When she fought for equality and refused to be submissive to her husband, she was cast out of paradise, and Eve was made from Adam's rib.

The patriarchy went on to say that Lilith was a crazed and evil woman, and to this day, they call her a demon. Lilith has been crucial in helping me unleash my inner wild and thrive in my truth. Take her story as a reminder to stay strong in your convictions, no matter how others project their insecurities onto you.

OCTOBER 4

It is important that we learn how to master our alignment with Self. We cannot control the actions of others or the grand plan of the Universe, but we *can* control how we respond to the varying factors in our lives.

We can shift our perspective whenever we choose to. This practice is not about moving forward blindly, ignoring situations that are unhealthy for our overall wellness. It is about recognizing what is not working in our lives and, instead of cycling through the same old negative-affirming thoughts, choosing positive-affirming ones. This is how we reach alignment with Self: by combining reality with higher spiritual wisdom and allowing this energy to carry us through all the ups and downs of our lives.

OCTOBER 5

Your thoughts are the most terrifying things that come up when you're trying to break a cycle. Your thoughts can be deceptive; they are powerful enough to keep you stuck where you are, even when you know better.

Take moments like these as an opportunity to find alignment and tune in to the truth of who you are. You have the power to transmute negativity into positivity, fear into trust, hate into love. Examine your negative thought patterns without getting attached to them. Become an observer instead of an active participant. Give your mind space to express itself without judgment. From your observational standpoint, enter the back of your mind. Submerge yourself in your subconscious and let the root causes of these thoughts make themselves known to you.

When you come back from your inner travels, take what you learned with you and use that wisdom to construct new, empowering thought forms. Be patient with your mind as you train it to work with your new beliefs, and be patient with your circumstances as they transition and you break the cycle once and for all.

OCTOBER 6

It's time to stop pointing fingers at everyone and everything but yourself. Your emotions and needs are no one else's responsibility but yours. To truly live, love, and thrive as an awakened, wise goddess, you must accept this truth now. Blaming and accusing others of what you perceive they are doing wrong will never solve your problems. It is up to you to take accountability and create change where you see fit.

Take accountability by accepting the role you have played in your circumstance. Take responsibility for the times you have stayed silent, the times you let mistreatment slide, the times you shrank yourself to fit into relationships and places you'd outgrown. Only you can move forward with the knowledge you have gained and apply it to your life. No one else is going to do it for you. Say what you want to say; demand respect. If your needs are still not being met, find someplace else where they will be. You have the power.

OCTOBER 7

You are the high priestess, the holder of ancient wisdom, the gatekeeper of life's mysteries. You can delve within your private world, your inner sanctuary at will. Draw on the prophecies you find inside to fuel your new seasons. Sacrifice your old ways of being to the Goddess and let yourself be reborn. Your understanding of what was and what is yet to come and your gentle surrender to the Wheel of Life are your superpowers. Be still, and let your soul lead you forward; patience breeds peace.

OCTOBER 8

When you lack clarity or fear that your desires are far out of reach, you may tend to feel lost. You are never truly lost, but in this dimension, you may perceive that you are, and this perception seems very real. In the darkness of misdirection, you are provided with an opportunity to turn to your inner compass: your intuition.

As you delve within, you'll find your intuition has been signaling which route to take since you began feeling lost. It's not that you were lost, but you were denying what your soul was telling you to do, creating the illusion of being lost.

Take back your power by honoring your intuition, emotions, and true desires. This is how you can redirect your course and find that sense of purpose again.

OCTOBER 9

Life is always giving you ample opportunities to choose love and develop your relationship with the Universe. Once in a blue moon, you may find yourself tangled in a cycle you thought you had previously healed. The Universe likes to provide chances to lean into faith and redefine love. You may feel like you're being tested when past issues come back into your life. In a way, you are being tested, but not in the way you think you're being tested.

The Universe never gives you anything you aren't equipped to handle. When old themes show up for you, the Universe is not saying, *You're not strong* or *You're being punished*. No. The Universe is simply reinforcing your resilience and ability to choose love over fear. Don't feel frustrated, and please do not feel unworthy. Instead, thank the Universe for reminding you of your own power and giving you another opportunity to shine your light and live in love.

OCTOBER 10

There are divine forces conspiring in your favor, always. Communication from the Divine comes through many different channels. You may receive intuitive nudges or have prophetic dreams, or someone else might give you a psychic reading. You may see the same words, symbols, or numbers again and again. Your loved ones deliver divine messages to you. Animals may cross your path to bring divine wisdom too. As you surrender and open yourself more deeply to divine intelligence and notice more and more signs and synchronicities appearing all around you, you might feel silly. Take comfort in the confirming nature of these occurrences. They come to you as sacred markers on your path, letting you know you are on the right track.

OCTOBER 11

Your experiences are yours and yours alone; no one can take them from you. The details of your memories may fade or become misconstrued as time rolls on, but the emotions you felt in those memories aren't likely to be forgotten. If you are at odds with someone over something that happened in the past, or if someone is trying to downplay your personal past experiences, let it go. You know what you felt, and you know how your experiences have shaped you. No one has the power to invalidate what you went through, whether they were there or not. What you've lived through and what you've learned are yours. Empower yourself with the lessons you've gained and the moments you have witnessed. You are wiser and stronger for each emotion and impact you have felt.

OCTOBER 12

Creating a spiritual practice that feels right to you can take time. And not only that, but your spiritual practice may also change many times throughout your life. There is a lot of literature about witchcraft, religions, and modern spiritual thought forms. Much of it provides brilliant insights and ideas for you to incorporate into your practice. I have seen many people ask about rules when it comes to studying tarot, taking up witchcraft, and building a spiritual practice. Let me tell you a not-so-secret secret: there are no rules.

Your spiritual practice is an expression of your soul. It is up to you to choose what kind of practice you'd like to build, what kind fits your soul best. There are certain things that should be brought into consideration when practicing. For example, rituals for drawing in new energies are generally best done when the moon is new or waxing. Things like this are good to keep in mind when developing your practice. But the most important thing is that your practice feels good to you. Learn what you can about the practices of others, taking what resonates and leaving the rest. You are meant to feel liberated by your practice and never confined.

OCTOBER 13

Karma is a force that governs your entire life. It is created in your past or present life and moves with you until you clear it. Karma can follow you forever unless you take the time to go within and heal yourself.

Earth is a school. You come here to experience life as a human, to learn, and to evolve as a soul. You make arrangements to rendezvous with other souls in your human experience. You create karma with others in a variety of ways. And if it is not corrected in your current experience, you will meet them in the next life with the intention of balancing your karma together.

When you feel that a connection or a situation no longer resonates with you, it is your duty to release it. If you try to hold on longer, ignoring the direction of your soul, you will block yourself from the blessings that are trying to make their way into your experience, and you will block karma from playing out. Answer the calling of your soul above all else, and root yourself in love. This is how you break karmic cycles.

OCTOBER 14

Nothing outside you will ever fill the void you feel within. You can search far and wide, but wherever you go, your emptiness will follow. It is your duty to explore yourself and address the root cause of your emptiness. What outdated beliefs are you operating from? What old wounds are still affecting you today? Find the courage to face them and heal them. You are wild, and you are complicated, but you are also wise and complete. You lack nothing. You have everything you need within you. You are the wounded warrior, and you are your own healer. Establish your relationship with yourself, build yourself up, and draw inspiration from the wonder that you are. Do not shrink in the face of the void. Use it as an opportunity for growth.

OCTOBER 15

Your confidence is attractive and highly magnetic. When you embody all three aspects of your Divine Feminine energy and free your inner goddess, everybody around you can sense and feel this. Through this process, you have reached a state of total alignment. In this space, everything you want finds its way to you with ease because you are confident in yourself, your power, and your connection to the Divine. If you are struggling to embrace and wear your confidence, spend time visualizing the woman you want to be. Let her image come through to you as she will. You're already her within. You just need to welcome her into your life and get to know her.

OCTOBER 16

Walking away because you know it's the right thing to do doesn't mean it is an easy thing to do. Where love, hard work, and lots of energy have been spent, walking away often feels like giving up. If you have given a situation your all and you still feel like you need to release it, know you are not giving up.

It becomes a question of worth. Are you valued where you are? Are you fulfilled? Does this situation *feel* right to you? These are the things you should ask yourself when faced with the decision to move on or stay put. If the answer to any of these questions is no, then you know what your next step is.

Love and honor yourself enough to make the right decision for you. You deserve to be fulfilled, respected, and loved wherever you are and wherever you go.

OCTOBER 17

Your intuition is designed to guide you to situations that will serve your highest good. This does not mean, however, that when listening to your intuition, you will only have good experiences.

Sometimes you may be guided to situations and relationships that are not meant to work out for you. This is because these things are destined to make a brief appearance in your life for the sole purpose of your learning a lesson. For example, you may feel strongly guided to apply for a certain job, or pursue a relationship with a certain someone, but it ultimately does not work out. You may feel angry when something you thought you wanted proves it wasn't all it was cracked up to be. Choose to look for deeper meaning, and you will find the silver lining. Every experience you have brings wisdom and serves your highest good.

OCTOBER 18

There is no need to attack anyone else for living the way they live. Everyone comes from the same Source energy. The reason you and others incarnate as humans is to evolve as souls. Since you are here for the purpose of evolution, you have your own lessons and experiences that you must go through and learn from. You have your own path to walk.

You may see someone living a life that simply doesn't feel right to you, and that's okay. They, like you, are trying to build a life that is authentic to them. Remind yourself that you don't have to make the same choices as they do and there is no reason for you to feel threatened by this contrast. Instead, examine why their way of doing things doesn't sit well with you. What is there for you to learn through the diversity of our planet?

OCTOBER 19

You carry within you the struggles, lessons, wisdom, and dreams that your ancestors held. Honor the headstrong and valiant people who came before you by lighting a white candle and sitting in silence for a few moments.

Pray to your ancestors for guidance and assistance. You are here to break generational cycles that have plagued your family for lifetimes. You are the one who was chosen to heal and rise in love. If at any time you find yourself struggling as you move through your own journey, invite your benevolent ancestors into your experience. They will support you as you find your strength and answer the calling of your soul.

OCTOBER 20

There is a stigma around change: that it is something chaotic and something to avoid if you can. But change is happening all the time, whether you recognize it or not. The hours change, the days change, the seasons change. What you eat and drink daily changes. What you wear changes. Nothing is ever exactly the same as it was before; stagnation is an illusion.

Take some time to think about all that has changed for you this year. How many wonderful changes did you accidentally overlook because you were looking for something bigger and better? What growth have you neglected to celebrate because you felt it was *not a big deal*?

Everything happens for a reason, and everything is intricately connected. You never know when one small change may be a catalyst for something huge to happen later.

OCTOBER 21

People fear what they don't understand. That's why the spiritual community, witches, lightworkers, and the occult are frowned upon. People outside these groups don't see the intention behind them. They think a witch is an evil woman and a lightworker lives in a fantasy world. What they're missing is that individuals who resonate with these titles are people who understand their own power. They are not afraid of the witches, lightworkers, and the rest. They're afraid of the responsibility that comes with developing their own source of power.

Being judged by someone who does not share your beliefs is nothing to be offended by. Keep focused on your own vibration and alignment, and let them walk their path.

OCTOBER 22

Orgasm is both death and creation. It is the physical embodiment of the energy that creates worlds. You can use your sexual power and climax to heal yourself, manifest your desires, and build intimacy with another. Through sexual acts, substantial amounts of energy are generated. When you surrender to pleasure, you activate your feminine energy. It is in this space where you are your most raw and vulnerable. It is your surrender and your full acceptance of all that you are that produces the power that creates life. Wield this energy to your advantage by directing it toward your desires. This is the wild feminine in her most liberated and empowered state.

OCTOBER 23

Half of intuition is observation. Your sixth sense is intuition. With your other five senses, you are simply observing the way something smells, looks, feels, tastes, or sounds. Your intuition is the sense that can perceive what is not easily observed with the other senses. Intuition is the observation of energy: the nonphysical.

Your intuition can pick up on someone's emotions or their intentions, or how a certain situation will play out. It can also utilize the other senses at times, such as smelling a "ghost scent" when connecting with the spirit world, for example, or hearing the voice of a spirit in your mind. This is what makes your intuition the ultimate superpower.

Intuition doesn't need to be hard to understand; it is simply another way of observing things, and it is a very natural part of being a human. The shifts happening on our planet largely rest on humanity's willingness to accept and hone the sixth sense.

OCTOBER 24

You unintentionally keep yourself stuck by dwelling on the past or anticipating the future. Bring your attention back to your present moment by focusing on all the wonderful things you have in your life. Notice how satisfying it is to eat delicious food, how comforting it is to feel the warmth of the sun on your face, or how safe you feel in your bed at night. Get in the habit of finding gratitude in your present moments, no matter how mundane they may seem at first. Through this practice, you weave the sacred into your daily life and embody gratitude, opening space for more blessings and abundance to enter.

OCTOBER 25

Just as wisdom can be passed down through generations, suffering can be too. Whether you are aware of it or not, there are patterns and cycles that have plagued your family for generations.

You are meant to break these cycles for good; it is your destiny. You do not have to carry the stories of your family and ancestors. It is your job to recognize these patterns and heal them and write your own story. As you do so, you free yourself and your family line. Don't let any old stories have power over you. Choose to rise above. By overcoming, you leave a new legacy for future generations to be inspired by.

OCTOBER 26

The feminine needs her freedom; she cannot stand any restraint. The commitment you've made to yourself beckons you to cut off the dead weight and rise in your power. Anything that is dragging you down is not needed where you're going. Anything that doesn't align with you is not worth your time.

Cleaning out the closet physically and mentally is what liberation is all about. Even if the thing you're clearing is something you once loved, if it's holding you back, it has served its purpose in your life. Free yourself with love and hold your head high as you move forward.

OCTOBER 27

If something you feel is meant to be a part of your experience consistently doesn't work out for you, you need to change your approach. Everything you experience is helping you learn more about who you are. Sometimes you may think you are acting from a place of alignment, but really, you are acting from a place of control. Whenever you force, you are not aligned. Whenever you control, you are grounded in fear.

All change starts within. If you want to see changes in your external world, you must begin by observing and improving your inner world. Ask yourself why this keeps not working for you. Are you rooted in love and alignment or fear and control? What lesson are you meant to learn? How can you adjust your mindset? How can you change your reaction, or lack thereof, to this situation?

OCTOBER 28

You hand your power over when you make decisions based on what you believe others would want you to do. I can think of a few things in my life that I regret solely because I chose to do what I *thought* someone else wanted—not what *I* wanted. These moments showed me the value of living the way I want to.

It's important to be respectful of people's feelings, yes. It's important to strive to follow the golden rule of treating others as you want to be treated. But when it comes down to it, if you want something for yourself that is different from what your companions want for you, you must find the strength within yourself to be a free spirit.

OCTOBER 29

The Dark Feminine reigns over night. She is not dark in her intention, but she honors the dark within. She is the alchemist, holding space for chaos and destruction, bitterness and vengeance. She does not act on her dark desires in the usual sense; she transmutes them into higher light. She places a shield around herself, her creations, and her loved ones, keeping the evil eye at bay. It is her energy that thrives when challenged and catapults you into unknown territory.

She is the symbol of rebirth, a beacon of new life. When you call upon her, be ready for change. Her love will wash over your entire being, purging the outdated from your system and clearing space for your desires to come in. Put your faith in her, and you will allow yourself to be transformed.

OCTOBER 30

Manipulation carries a different vibration from manifestation. When you manipulate, you sell yourself short. Manipulation is an attempt to control a situation and does not come from a place of power; it is rooted in deception. Manifestation is co-creation with the Universe and only works if it comes from real power; it is rooted in truth.

When you try to manipulate, you affirm you do not feel worthy of what you want, and you must trick your desired outcome into being. Manipulating says you do not trust Source to bring you everything you want and need.

When you manifest, you affirm that you deserve your desires, and you trust they will come into being in a way that serves your highest good. Manifestation is more open and fluid and less controlled than manipulation. Manifestation helps you align with love—love for yourself, love for others, and love for the Divine.

Before you set out to manifest or perform a ritual, ensure you are moving with peace, not distortion. If you have intentionally manipulated a situation before, forgive yourself, for you were only acting from a wound. Take accountability and align your energy to attract your new desires from a place of authenticity.

OCTOBER 31

Samhain, known as summer's end to the ancient Celts and Halloween in our modern day, is the third harvest festival on the Wheel of the Year. This sabbat symbolizes the death element of the ever-unfolding life, death, and rebirth cycle that governs nature. On this day, the omnipresent Goddess in her Crone form mourns the omnipresent God when he passes into the underworld. The sun's power has waned, and the nights are growing longer. Winter is approaching, and we are called to introspection.

Reflect on what parts of your existence are ready for the release of death. In solitude, identify thoughts, habits, and parts of yourself that are ready to be transformed. The first step to this process is acceptance.

Accept where you are, who you are, and how your needs have changed over the year. Know that the bittersweet experience of death is a natural and necessary part of the growth cycle. To be reborn anew, you must sacrifice that which stands in your way, even if its presence once brought comfort and security. Lean into the wisdom of your inner Crone as you acknowledge all you must release to rise again come spring.

NOVEMBER 1

Following Samhain, the omnipresent energies of Divine Feminine and Divine Masculine are declining. The God has retired, and the Goddess mourns his loss. The sun's presence is noticeably shorter, and each night is longer and colder than the last. As a collective, we are spending much more time indoors, keeping warm amid the changing weather. This is a time of slowing down, as our inner masculine energy is less active, and your inner feminine is more reflective. The Earth seems to stand still as you consider where you've been and where you are going. Whatever energy you find yourself in as the year begins to wind down, remember to be gentle with yourself. There is a rhythm to all things, and the time for rich activity and glorious expansion will come again.

NOVEMBER 2

Become acquainted with your own energy so you know when you are being affected by energy that is not yours. Throughout the day, you may come into contact with many other people who have also been in contact with many people. Information is always coming at you, whether it be from one-on-one conversation, television, or social media. Unknowingly, you may absorb some of the energy thrown at you. Adopting a foreign energy as your own can mess with your vibration and your overall wellness.

To get to know your energy better, spend time in solitude every day. Reflect and go within. Examine your inner world, and get a clear picture of your truth. When you know your truth, you can easily identify when you are being influenced by the energy of another.

NOVEMBER 3

Be aware of what is—not consumed by it. Hyper-focusing on circumstances in your life that are dissatisfying does nothing but rob you of your power. The more energy you give to something, the greater its power grows because you are handing your essence over to the situation.

Reclaim your power by changing the thoughts you are holding. Align with love, and redirect fear-based thoughts.

Recognize the power you have within you, and shift the energy of the situation. As you adjust your thought patterns and consciously direct your energy, you will find two things happen: One, you will feel sustained because you are no longer giving your energy to something you don't want, and you have found peace with what is. Two, you will see what you do want to manifest in your reality.

NOVEMBER 4

There is a stigma connected with fear: that it is an emotion we should keep to ourselves and deny. Fear is at the opposite end of the same pole as love. Although it isn't pleasant to feel, it is a part of our human paradigm, and it is a great teacher from whom we can gain a lot of wisdom.

Whenever fear is active within us, we are provided an opportunity to peel back another layer of ourselves. With practice, we can sit with our fears and begin to understand them, and in time, fear will not freeze us but will empower us to rise.

Because our life experience is nonlinear, some of our fears may visit again after we have worked through them. But if we continue to see fear as a teacher and look for the message intertwined within a particular fear, we will prevail time and time again. Fear is the key to our strengths. We need both fear and love to be whole.

NOVEMBER 5

Detach and allow. It is not your job to dictate what others do with their time and energy. Your mission is to live a life that is authentic to you, not meld others into the perfect vision you have for them. If your intention is to "trigger" people into their healing, stop where you are and reflect. You are not meant to control others; you are meant to lead with love and acceptance. Release the desire to shape others into who you think they should be, and instead hold space for them to grow into their full potential.

NOVEMBER 6

Sin is nothing but rhetoric designed by mainstream religion to control and inflict conformity. In everything we do, there are choices, and it is true that one choice may be better or more karmically correct than another. In everything we experience, we will feel a multitude of emotions. But the choices we regret are not innately bad, and neither are the various emotions we feel. When we feel compelled to do something, we feel that way for a reason. And when we observe an emotion we're feeling, we will find that it is an expression of something else going on within us.

Our culture denies that everyone is unique in their perception of the world and the human experience. We are not here to live identical lives. We are here to collect experiences and gain spiritual wisdom, which we are meant to apply to our lives moving forward. We must do what we feel called to do, we must honor the way we feel, and we must challenge the construct put forth by religion. This is how we learn and grow.

NOVEMBER 7

Anxiety is the language of fear. It can be simply an expression of fear, but it can also be a signal that you are out of alignment. Anxiety arrives to make you aware that you are believing the opposite of what your soul knows to be true, or continuing a path that does not suit you.

You can influence and shift your anxiety by calling your energy back to yourself. Remember your power, and know that you have control over your thoughts and actions. Tune in to your own spirit, and release the desire to control situations that are outside your control. Focus on what you can control and leave the rest up to Source. Surrendering to a path that is in alignment with your core truth can ease anxiety and reignite your lust for life.

NOVEMBER 8

You are a divine channel. Your awareness and the activation of your Divine Feminine energy allow you to pull wisdom from the cosmos as needed. Call on the Goddess when you need guidance. Let her fill you with love and pour her light into you. No matter what you have done, no matter who you have been, you deserve happiness, love, and blessings in your life. She is always with you, and she is always ready to show you the path to your greatest liberation and enlightenment. Ask for her help, and be open to receiving her assistance.

NOVEMBER 9

All is cyclical. The moon goes through the same phases each month, and the seasons shift in the same way, in the same order, each year. Your life behaves in the same way. There will be familiar faces, familiar lessons, and familiar experiences. Revisiting the old is not meant to discourage you. It is only meant to serve as a reflection of how much you have grown. Sometimes you may find you still have more work to do. At other times you may find that you understand the lesson and can move on quickly. In any case, respect the rhythms and cycles of your mind, body, and spirit. Respect the flow of life, and accept that patterns are natural. There is nothing wrong with you. You cannot mess up your path.

NOVEMBER 10

If you find yourself in a displeasing repetitive cycle that never seems to end, remember how much power you truly hold and take accountability for the role you are playing in this situation. You do not have to stick to any situation or old desire that no longer resonates with the person you are becoming. You can enter a new reality at any time by adjusting your approach.

You don't have to know all the answers or what moves to make. Do some soul searching and discover what you are craving and how your needs are changing. When you know, align your thoughts and energy with the way you want to feel or with what you want to experience. Follow up by taking action in your physical world. Surrender to the timing of your life, and allow your new reality to form.

NOVEMBER 11

Navigating your inner world is a beautiful and other-worldly experience. Within your inner sanctum, you will find both bliss and misery. Sometimes you will want to stay inside your inner realms for hours on end and embrace the light that resides there. At other times you will want to run from yourself and never go within ever again because of the darkness there. Both are normal responses.

But to be all that you are is to know all that you are. To know enlightenment, to thrive in your feminine power, you must get to know both the light and dark goddesses within. Each has a voice, and each of these voices has been suppressed by you or another over the course of your experience. To find yourself and to find your way, listen to the wisdom both have to share. Create a good balance, one that works for you, between the two. Then you will know how a full heart feels.

NOVEMBER 12

Feminine love needs to be tough sometimes. At some point, you must be real with yourself. You must acknowledge when you are settling. You must own your mistakes. You must take responsibility for your actions and where they have led you. You must make the choice to move differently if you want different experiences.

As life is cyclical, you will have many lessons that help you access your authentic power. You will revisit time and time again how to stand in your authenticity and speak from your own voice. You will be given thousands of chances to move more deeply into alignment and find your truth again.

Hold yourself accountable. Know when it is time for you to change your way of being. Speak those harsh truths; bring them into the light with you. Accept when it is time to change, and do not hold yourself back.

NOVEMBER 13

Sometimes things happen that you just can't explain. Things don't go the way you planned or hoped. Things fall apart. And as much as you want to understand why, some part of you knows you will never have that satisfaction. That employer will never tell you why they didn't see you as fit for the job. The weather won't divulge why it chose to delay your plans. That person will never give you a good enough reason for their behavior or their absence. But if you are patient and if you trust, Spirit will reveal why things had to be this way in time. When in doubt, let go. Surrender the desire to go back and fix things. Pray for an outcome that serves the highest good of all. Things that are unclear will be illuminated someday. Release the need to know, and turn your focus inward. Anything that is blocked from you is protection from Spirit. Anything that leaves your life will be replaced by something better.

NOVEMBER 14

Your intuition is the solemn voice of your inner Crone. It is the eternal part of you that holds your wisdom. Here, you will find valuable insights from all your past lives, and everything you have experienced in your current life cycle.

Your intuition is there to guide you, not sway you. It is there to assist you so you can make choices in your life that will truly serve your highest good.

When you trust your inner Crone and follow her guidance, you will always be guided to whomever and whatever will serve you the best.

NOVEMBER 15

No one is keeping you stuck except you. Everyone reflects you to yourself, whether it be in a personal relationship, your professional relationships, or the relationship you have with society and government. You have a voice, you have ideas, and you have the ability to free yourself and change your life for the better. Do not let any outside influences keep you from doing what you really want to do. Doing so is just making excuses for yourself. Rise in your power, and take charge.

NOVEMBER 16

When you're tuned in to your psychic abilities, the truth becomes evident, regardless of words. Words and language can be beautiful, but energy says so much more. It's the energy of a person that draws you to them. It's the energy of a place that makes you feel like you want to be there. Pay attention to the subtleties in the energy of the places you visit and the people you rendezvous with. Let yourself get swept away by the energies you adore, and choose to honor your soul's desires when an energy doesn't feel right to you. Energy always speaks for itself and is the true language of the soul.

NOVEMBER 17

Overlooked lessons will follow you into new situations until you have integrated the wisdom being shown to you. All change must first happen within. Then the Universe can come through with its guiding hand and assist you with changing your external world.

Moving from one location to another, whether it be toxic relationships, negative working environments, or unsatisfactory homes, will not make the underlying issue go away. If you miss the lessons provided by these circumstances, the lessons will move with you as you jump from situation to situation. Go within yourself to find out why these patterns are repeating for you. Connect with your higher mind and you will gain clarity. Once the truth is unveiled and integrated by you, you will be free from repeated patterns.

NOVEMBER 18

It's okay to mourn the end of an era. It's normal to cry and feel nervous. You are allowed to grieve, even if you are the one making the choice to leave. Many things stay behind when you choose to release what no longer serves you; identities, relationships, environments, routines are among them. If, however, you make the conscious choice to bring with you the love and the lessons learned, you will leave better than you were when you got there. Endings and changes bring growth. Best of all, they bring your answered prayers. Never stay in a situation that is stifling your development out of fear of the unknown. Take the leap of faith, and clear space for new blessings to come pouring in.

NOVEMBER 19

When the Egyptian goddess Isis learned the name of Ra, her enemy, she had power over him. His darkness could no longer control her, for she knew the name of the game. This is how we must begin looking at the limitations we have within ourselves.

We all have flaws. We all have some conditioning or beliefs that keep us from reaching our full potential. The reason they keep us from rising is not that they have the power to do so on their own. It is because we hand our power over to them when we ignore them or let them keep us stuck. When we learn their name, they lose all power.

You must go within to discover the name of your darker inner energies so they can no longer control you.

NOVEMBER 20

Well-being is a state created from knowing and honoring the self. We are primal creatures; we have natural instincts that move us forward. We have dreams and visions for our future, and we have aspirations and longings that demand fulfillment. When we ignore these inner callings, we deny ourselves well-being.

We can wear masks. We can pretend that we are happy with settling. But the longer we stay in places that do not resonate with us, the more our mind, body, and soul suffer. Denying our true emotions and needs eventually creates a physical imbalance within the body. This is when illness and disease appear. As we age, we must remember to check in with ourselves. Are we being true to our inner goddess, or are we denying some aspect of ourselves? When we bring ourselves into alignment by honoring what we feel inside, our well-being will maintain itself.

NOVEMBER 21

The Principle of Polarity states that everything has two extremes; a high and a low. For example: rich and poor, healthy and unhealthy, purity and impurity. As a vibrational being, you oscillate between the varying poles present in your life. One day you may maintain a vibration that aligns you with abundance, but if a surprise bill shows up, you may drop down to a vibration that is closer to a lack mentality.

In everything you do, remember to take time out to reflect upon your intentions and vibration. Go within to see if you are making decisions from a place of love and empowerment, or a place of fear and the desire to control. Observing and realigning your vibration regularly helps you stay on the path that serves your highest good. It's okay if you need to adjust your vibration; you're human and are doing the best you can. Just remember who you are, and check yourself when needed.

NOVEMBER 22

If you cannot muster the energy to have faith in yourself, let faith in the Divine be enough. Surrender your worries to Spirit; let go of what you have been clinging to so tightly. Create space in your heart and mind for solutions to come forward—and they will. Sometimes the plan you had for your life is intercepted by the plan Spirit has for you. The act of letting go automatically moves you out of your own way, so the Divine can continue to move you where it sees fit. No matter how dark the path ahead may seem, choose to have faith. Your future is bright.

NOVEMBER 23

In this world both light and dark exist, and that's just the way it is. Talking about the New Age we are birthing conjures ideas of a world where there is absolutely no negativity. It's true that we are sowing fertile soil from which a healthier planet will be born, but our goal should never be to erase negativity altogether.

Remember, without the darkness, there is no light. We need the dark times to challenge us, to be catalysts for growth. We need the darkness because it helps us discern who we really are and what is truly important to us.

The new world is not one built upon false positivity but one in which we thrive in our darkness and our light.

NOVEMBER 24

A change of scenery almost always brings a fresh perspective. When you put yourself in new spaces, you allow new information to reach you. Being out of your comfort zone, and what is known to you, helps you reflect upon the concerns you have left back home, without feeling the realness or stagnancy of them. Sometimes all you need is to shake up your routine. You'll return home with a new approach and revitalized energy, well prepared to tackle the challenges you are facing.

NOVEMBER 25

The more you trust your intuition, the more accurate she becomes. If you treat her like the girl who cried wolf, why would you expect her to get stronger? And if doubting her has never helped you before, why don't you try giving her a chance? I think you'll find that just going with her will often prove you right. Listen to her. She has good answers for you.

NOVEMBER 26

When you feel closed off and exhausted, and keep walls around your heart, you are experiencing an imbalance between your masculine and feminine energies. Your inner masculine seeks to protect you and doesn't have an easy time tuning in to your emotions and intuition. Operating too heavily in your masculine energy while your feminine fades into the background can create a plethora of problems for you. To bring these energies back into balance, slow down, ground yourself in your present moment, and find ways to nurture yourself. Tell yourself it is safe for you to feel your emotions and it is natural for you to utilize your intuition. Assure yourself that you are worthy of giving and receiving love and that you deserve to express your wants and needs in your relationships. There is no need to put up walls of protection, for you are here to experience love in all its forms.

NOVEMBER 27

You don't have to meditate daily, know all the crystals, or own a tarot deck to be spiritual. You are spiritual by nature, as you come from Source. The point of having a spiritual practice is to spend time with your own soul and build upon your innate connection with the Divine. All you need is intention and a willingness to devote time to yourself, your soul, and Spirit. The ways in which you choose to dedicate time to your practice need to be in alignment with your truth. Don't force anything if it doesn't fit. The methods that are meant for you will feel easy and right.

NOVEMBER 28

One of the hardest things to accept about life is that it comes with pain. No one likes to admit this, and even when it is admitted, the person saying it is not usually in a lot of pain when they say it. People always mean well when they say that you must experience the bad times to recognize the good ones. And although this is true, the sentiment rarely helps much.

Heartbreak is one of those elusive feelings—everyone feels it and deals with it in a different way. No way is wrong, but some ways may be healthier than others.

The first step to feeling better is accepting that you are feeling pain. It is okay for you to feel whatever you are feeling. Your emotions are your own, so don't let them be stifled because they are making someone else uncomfortable. Allow your emotions to have full rein for a little while. When you do this, you will be freed and the steps toward healing will become clearer.

NOVEMBER 29

Throughout your life you make vows and share your sacred essence with many souls. If the energy you give is not reciprocated in a healthy way, your soul essence can break into fragments. When you feel blocked, or like you are unable to see success in certain areas of your life, it could be because those lost parts of your essence are still missing from your energy.

When you feel powerless, tune in to your body, focusing on the parts within that feel empty. Call your power and essence back from all spaces. You may see images in your mind of people and places of the past, moments your power was left behind in. Visualize the parts of you that feel empty being filled with the light of Source. See your power flowing back into your aura and body and know you have retrieved your lost energy.

NOVEMBER 30

If something is not manifesting in your life now, that doesn't mean it never will. Sometimes it's a question of faith, and at other times it's a question of fate. You may need to build up your self-worth, your belief in yourself, and your trust in the Divine before your dream can manifest. Conversely, what you're desiring may not be a part of your life plan at the current juncture—it may come at a later stage, or it could come in another form than the one you had hoped for. Be open to the blessings that want to come into your life, even if they are different from what you had originally asked for. The Goddess knows what is best for her children; let her bring you the gifts that will best serve you.

DECEMBER 1

Each Crone season brings with it a period of massive death and rebirth throughout the collective. You may revisit things you buried long ago, things you thought you had healed and moved past. It may feel disheartening, but rest assured—whatever is coming up for you now is being brought to your awareness so you can transmute it, creating space for the new in the process.

Be gentle with yourself and others. Don't be so quick to jump to conclusions or take anything too personally. The darkness of winter is approaching, and it means business. Anything exiting from your journey right now is not meant to go with you into the new year. Lean into faith, surrendering deeper with each passing day. Let go and trust.

DECEMBER 2

You cannot erase the past, and you shouldn't spend your energy wishing you could. Your experiences helped make you the person you are today. Without them, you wouldn't know who you are and you would never know your own strength. You rise from the ashes of your past, like the phoenix. If the ashes didn't exist, where would you rise from?

DECEMBER 3

The answers to our questions are so simple that we often overlook them. Simple, yet profound. Most center around choosing love, trust, and faith more than anything else. We get in our own way by trying to figure out each little detail. We have become creatures of comfort, wanting safety and security guaranteed before we make a move. Life doesn't work that way. It is not our job to worry about each step on our journey. If we were meant to know the exact milestones of our life plan, and how to get to them, we would remember those details upon incarnating. But we don't remember them. Those details are for Spirit to handle. Our duty is only to get closer to our own Source. As we do that, the path becomes clearer.

DECEMBER 4

Peace is created through your trust in yourself and the Divine. With any challenge or adversity that comes your way, strive to see things from the eyes of your inner goddess. She knows that all is well, and that everything that is occurring is perfectly right for you. This can be difficult to accept unless you already feel within that it is time for a change. But even still, it can be hard to flow through transition, as your ego wants to worry and pause time.

Choose to see every heavy situation in your life from a higher perspective. There is a reason for every hurt, every ending, and every loss. More often than not, the reason is to redirect you and make space for a new blessing to enter. Find peace in knowing that you are being taken care of, and that there is a purpose to everything you experience. You are safe, and you are being guided, always. Let yourself mourn what was, and let yourself be in the darkness for a while, knowing that the sun will rise again.

DECEMBER 5

Push yourself through your barriers; break through your limitations. There is nothing you cannot do. Your thoughts may tell you something different, but your higher mind knows the truth. Life continues to roll on. Things that seem huge today may not even matter to you in six months' time. Moments you don't dwell upon may prove to be some of the most important in your life. No matter what, you will always be okay. You will always have the chance to start again. Time is an illusion; age is a natural part of living, not a reason not to live. Move past limited thinking, and jump out of your comfort zone. Be unruly; try something new. Let yourself enjoy the things you draw into your experience, regardless of how they *end up*. It's never really the end; you are eternal. Take a chance.

DECEMBER 6

Life moves in patterns and cycles, both for individuals and the collective. If we observe our own history, as well as the collective's, we will notice many repetitive patterns playing out. It's important that we preserve the stories that have shaped us because when we are in need at a crossroads, we can always look to the past to help us decide what the future will be.

We are birthing a time of greater balance in our world right now. Looking at humanity's past, it is clear which paths we'd like to avoid and which may provide us with a strong foundation for the future.

DECEMBER 7

Be so secure in yourself that you don't feel the need to put another down. Power does not come from projecting. Passing judgment on another does nothing but lower your vibration and disturb your inner peace. Give others the space to be themselves and make their own choices. Their decisions do not impact you, and their actions only have power over you if you allow them to. Make inner peace your priority, and choose to love with an open heart and mind.

DECEMBER 8

Rising requires devotion to all that you are and acceptance of the parts of you that you're compelled to control. Everyone has flaws and traits they find easier to accept than others. Everyone has made mistakes on their path that they are not proud of. The desire to bury your head in the sand when you've done something wrong is tempting, but this is the time you need to love yourself even more. Hold your head up high, and take accountability for the role you played to get you where you are. Instead of damning yourself for your mistakes, recognize the impact they have had on your evolution. Understand that your flaws need to be acknowledged and worked with, not ridiculed and ignored. Be aware that your flaws cannot have power over you when you know their name. Move forward with grace and dignity, accepting all of yourself, giving power to your positive traits and loving the ones on the opposite end of the same pole.

DECEMBER 9

There's no sugarcoating the unbearable pain that comes when you miss someone you love. It's so overwhelming, yet so indescribable. And even though it's something all people experience, you may feel as if no one can understand your pain.

You may miss people for varying reasons, so there is no one, superior way to get through it. Never mind the things that were left unsaid, or the moments you wish your loved ones could share with you in the present.

During the throes of loss, turn to your spiritual practice. You are not your physical body; you are your soul. You are never really separated from anyone you love because you are always together in spirit. Even if the person you're missing is someone with whom you've only lost contact, know that the eternal parts of you still feel that same love you once shared in person. Whether you're missing someone in the physical or the nonphysical world, know that your souls will be reunited someday—in this life or the next.

DECEMBER 10

The Divine gifts you with blessings that are meant just for you. The ideas you receive are meant for you to explore. There will be times when you feel frozen by imposter syndrome, and you will ask yourself if you are good enough to fulfill the divine tasks that are sent to you. Although you have free will, remember, the Divine sends you only what you can handle. If an opportunity or idea shows up for you, it is meant for you. Know that you are more than good enough, and if you choose to follow through, you will be blessed beyond measure.

DECEMBER 11

Winter comes, an icy crone, whispering her musings with her chilled breath. There's a sense in the air that magic is around every corner and things could change in an instant. It's a great time to take stock: What have you harvested this year? What is stored away for later use? What has long served its purpose?

As the winter solstice approaches and the sun is reborn, tune in to your inner light to carry you into the new year. Rejoice in the love, abundance, and joy that have filled your heart throughout this season, and all seasons prior. Celebrate the fresh energy flowing into your experience.

The cycle is soon to begin again. You are ready.

DECEMBER 12

You travel through life with a team of spirit guides, angels, and ancestors who are always with you and waiting for you to call on them. They send you signs about your path; they encourage you, and they love you. Sometimes their love may feel a little tough, but they always have your highest good in mind. Make it a point to connect with these beings by practicing meditation, divination, or even automatic writing.

Whenever you are in need, they will be there to support you. Ask them to communicate with you in your dreams, in waking life, and through specific signs of your choosing. They are happy to assist, as their sole purpose is to help you rise and thrive.

DECEMBER 13

As the energy of the old wanes, as the energy of the new gains momentum, the space in between can feel like it's never going to change at all. These are the moments when you must allow yourself to drop into surrender. The space in between what's dead and what's about to be reborn is sacred. It is in this space where you can tune in to your inner worlds and contemplate what your soul is yearning for. It is here you find solace amid chaos and peace amid confusion. In the space in between, establish gratitude for what has been and for what's to come. What was will never be again, and what's coming is your answered prayer.

DECEMBER 14

Women don't really fear getting older; they fear being of no value. They fear having no spark—nothing left to say, no new adventures, and retiring into a parody of ourselves. Women especially have been programmed to believe there are certain milestones they are expected to reach, and once each one has been checked off the list, there's nothing left to live for. It's time to collectively change the narrative.

The sooner you can establish self-worth, the better. Valuing yourself prevents society from diminishing you. In hindsight, age doesn't matter. It is never too late to create new experiences for yourself. Until your last breath, you have the power to manifest the life you love. You are invaluable. Don't give up on you.

DECEMBER 15

It's okay to feel lower vibrational emotions. It's okay to feel sad, scared, angry, and even hopeless. Modern spirituality and mindfulness practices often promote positivity and wellness mindsets. You should always strive to be more positive and think thoughts that feel good to you, but toxic positivity is also very real. Being mindful doesn't mean always being positive; it means being mindful of *everything* that is happening within you.

Allow yourself to feel all your emotions. Sit with yourself; acknowledge how you really feel. Even if it is a time when you feel that you *should* be feeling happy or excited but you truly feel sad or overwhelmed—sit with it. Allow your emotions to communicate with you.

And when you feel you have honored this part of yourself, try to move on. All emotions deserve to be felt, but not all should be dwelt upon.

DECEMBER 16

The winds of winter might remind you of the importance of solitude. When it's cold outside and the air element is active, you may feel inspired to reflect upon the year behind you and fantasize about the one ahead. As you delve into your inner spaces, you can begin to see more clearly what you have been housing that doesn't serve you. Utilize the wind energy to clear out anything that doesn't belong to you. Your mental spaces can get so crowded with the voices and emotions of others; you must discern what is coming with you as you prepare to be reborn in the new year. Allow the wind to carry away what you no longer need. Release your grasp and throw caution to the wind.

DECEMBER 17

There is nothing you can do to cause your feminine gifts to disappear, and everything you can do to enhance them. The collective has been operating primarily from masculine energy for ages as feminine energy slept, waiting to be awakened.

There's no need to worry that you aren't intuitive or that you can't be creative. You already have these and many more magical gifts within. You don't need to force yourself to follow specific rituals or only eat certain diets in order to access your innate gifts. All you need to do is make the conscious decision to tune in with your soul and do things that feel good to you.

Eat the foods your body prefers, meditate in a way that makes sense for you, and be creative in ways that feel natural and right to you. Listen to your body, and pay attention to your own vibration, always. If something feels good to you, keep it in your life; if not, release it. You are spiritual by nature, and nothing can take that away from you. Craft your life the way you want it to be, and you will always feel connected to Source.

DECEMBER 18

Through your experiences, you can be a guiding light to others. Your life is as unique as your soul. What you have lived through is yours. There will always be others who can relate to your story and whose stories you can relate to. Yet no one lives the exact same life as another. You have so much to offer those who are like you—and those who are unlike you. Shining your light for all to see brings inspiration and change where needed. Instead of fearing what will happen if you reveal your true self to the world, fear what will happen if you don't. Get out there and let your voice be heard.

DECEMBER 19

Our culture takes pride in its version of strength, which usually entails overworking ourselves, denying our emotions, and ignoring our souls' calling in order to serve the system's agenda. For this reason, we rarely ask for help when we need it. We would rather push ourselves to the point of breaking than ask another to help lighten our load. This puts a real damper on our energy levels and hardens our hearts. Real strength lies in the ability to decipher when it is time to slow down, soften, and honor the needs of our body and soul. We must let people in and ask for help when we need it. We do not need to prove ourselves to anyone.

DECEMBER 20

Ground yourself in your Crone aspect when solitude calls. There is a well of wisdom lying within you that wishes to be given a voice. Your Crone aspect will oversee your inner travels, providing guidance and support when needed. Activate your inner knowing through stillness, silence, prayer, and divination. Be open to receiving new perspectives, answers to your questions, and advice regarding where to take your journey next. Your Crone energy understands that life is fluid, always changing and moving into new cycles. Her faith and certainty show you the way when the path ahead seems dark. Embrace her insights and be comforted by knowing that what she shares with you is exactly what you need at the moment. Accept her wisdom, and go on with grace.

DECEMBER 21

Yule, from the winter solstice until January 1, marks the rebirth of the omnipresent God, or Divine Masculine energy. This is the second solar sabbat on the Wheel of the Year, and after this day, the sun will gradually grace us with its presence for longer and longer each day, until it reaches its peak at Litha, the summer solstice, when it will begin to retire once more. Thus the winter solstice is the longest night of the year.

At Yule, the Goddess temporarily shifts out of her Crone archetype and into her Mother energy so she may birth the God (the sun) back into the world, as his energy began waning after the Mabon. This is a promise the Goddess made during Beltane, in the spring. She will return to her Crone form for the majority of winter, before embodying her Maiden energy once more come Imbolc.

DECEMBER 22

Embrace stillness. Every answer you could ever seek, every truth you need to hear already lies within you. The more time you spend on your own, in the silence of your own essence, the more you come to understand yourself. With the understanding of the self comes the understanding of others and your place in the world.

No longer will you feel the need to seek validation from the mouth of someone else. No longer will you scroll social media for a sign. The comfort of your own certainty becomes enough to move you forward. And when synchronicities appear on your path, the appreciation you feel will come from a place of confirmation of what you already know.

DECEMBER 23

Any choice made in love is the right one to make. You will be reborn countless times throughout your life. With each rebirth, you will expand your capacity to love. It is love that guides your way, leading you to your highest timelines. When given the choice to start anew or stay where you are, always observe where the energy of love is flowing. If it is moving in a new direction, that is the one you are meant to follow, even if you are afraid. If it is staying where you are, that is where you are meant to be. Making authoritative decisions rooted in love will always bring blessings and karmic rewards into your life. Every time you act in love, you help make the world a better place.

DECEMBER 24

You can never know what someone else is going through until you have walked a mile in their shoes. It is your mission as an activated Divine Feminine to be the light for others, whether you know them personally or not. As you heal, others heal. As you shine your inner light, the light in others switches on. When you choose to love, you make the world a better place. Day by day, the more love you spread, the more love wins. Choose love and acceptance over hate and judgment every time.

DECEMBER 25

Source expresses itself through life, and spirituality is the language used. Life is a play in which to enact spiritual concepts. Spirituality isn't all love and light. Like spirituality, life is not all fluff either. To connect with your soul and understand the totality of who you are, to have a complete human experience, you must become acquainted with both the light and shadow of life and spirituality.

DECEMBER 26

The solstices on the Wheel of the Year beautifully depict the symbiotic relationship between the Earth's two hemispheres and the omnipresent Divine Feminine energy. In the Southern Hemisphere, the summer solstice is occurring, while those in the Northern experience the winter solstice. This means the Goddess in the Southern Hemisphere is embodying her Mother archetype while the Goddess in the Northern Hemisphere is embodying her Crone aspect. The sun is laid to rest in the Southern Hemisphere, just as it is being born in the Northern and vice versa. With each solstice, the Mother and Crone temporarily fulfill each other's duties on opposite sides of the world, greatly showcasing the intricacy of the Goddess's impact on our planet and her limitless presence. Her love carries us throughout the year, and it is so vast that she will become whatever she needs to be for us to behold the experiences we need.

DECEMBER 27

The word *forever* carries so much pressure with it. People will ask you, "Is this where you want to be *forever*?"

More emphasis needs to be put on the *now*. Is this where you want to be now? Are you happy? Are you fulfilled? What can you do to make your now experience more pleasing? Focus on that, and leave forever to the Divine.

DECEMBER 28

As the year ends and this chapter of your life closes, welcome peace into your being. As you face the dawning of a new day, remember who you are: a wise goddess. Continue to deepen your connection with Source through your connection with yourself. Lean into this connection whenever you need extra love and support. Trust, and know you are always being guided and protected. Seek the magical moments in each day. Tune in to gratitude; welcome more abundance and blessings into your experience. Allow your youthful spirit to fuel your passions, your wholeness to illuminate your path, and your shadow to provide contrast. Take aligned action, speak your truth, and utilize your innate power to craft the life you love every day. You are a divine spark of light; you are love. Hold this wisdom in your heart and allow it to be your strength in all that comes your way.

DECEMBER 29

It is human nature to pretend everything is okay when it's not, always praising the higher times in life and acting as though the lows are nonexistent.

To be a complete being and live a full life, you must accept that both the dark and the light exist on this plane. Heavier moments are so necessary because they act as guidance for you. Without sadness, you wouldn't seek happiness. Without discomfort, you would not strive for more. Without fear, you would never know love.

The walk of life is nonlinear; you will experience an array of energies and emotions as long as you live. Honor the times when you are not feeling your best. Allow yourself to fully experience your emotions and delve into what they are trying to show you. Know that the darkness will not last forever, illusions will fade, and the path ahead will light up, bringing in a brand new cycle once more.

DECEMBER 30

Time is an illusion, yet the wheel is always turning. Divine timing is a constant in life. The soul knows this, but the mind wants to know all the answers and how everything will play out. The mind seeks a false sense of security. But the heart knows security comes from having faith. All the answers lie within you, and they call out to you when you embrace stillness and plant yourself in your present moment. There is no need to rush and no need to force. Take it easy and remember to enjoy your journey. As the wheel turns, nothing is ever the same again. Fill your body with gratitude, for one day you will only be able to reminisce about today.

DECEMBER 31

Break out of the mold that binds you. Dare to challenge what has come before. Take life by the reins and don't ever stop claiming what is yours. You are a Divine Feminine. You can never be contained; you can never be restricted. You are a force that moves mountains, births worlds. You are a sacred wisdom-keeper, the bearer of change, the messenger of the Divine. Get out there and do what you must do: travel, take risks, start again, love, cry, win, lose. Throughout it all, continue to choose to rise. As you move in the name of authenticity, you serve your soul's mission. Liberating yourself, you liberate humanity. Loving yourself, you inspire others to love themselves. Finding your Source guides others to theirs. Always be you. You are the chosen one.

CLOSING WORDS

The path of the Goddess is wild and untamed, as is her nature. Hers is an energy that cannot be contained by the constructs of human language; rather, she is felt in the beating of our hearts, the blood in our veins, the deepest parts of our psyche. She meets us at a visceral level and illuminates the path to our greatest fulfillment. She cannot be captured, cannot be forced, and cannot be faked. She is to be sensed, embraced, and embodied.

When we make the choice to step into our Divine Feminine essence, we not only empower ourselves but we also empower everyone we meet. As we all own our authenticity, hone our magic, and spread love, we heal our ancestral line and families, we heal our communities, and we change the course of humanity for the better.

You have taken on a role of great importance. It takes strength to go within, heal yourself, and rise again. Take this moment to celebrate yourself and to honor all that you are and how far you have come.

The path of the Divine Feminine is not always easy. There will be moments when you feel restless, hopeless, and unable to connect with your true self. The journey is cyclical; you will revisit feelings you have felt before, and you will be refreshed on lessons previously learned. You will be challenged in new ways, and you will sometimes find it hard to see the light.

In the varying highs and lows of your path, remember the medicine brought forth by each of her archetypes. Draw from your inner Maiden when it's time to be daring, embody your inner Mother when it is time to be compassionate, and delve into your inner Crone when you need clarity. If you flow with her, you will continuously unlock new levels of appreciation and understanding of yourself and the world around you.

It is up to you to allow the goddess within to emerge, for as you do, you create a new golden age on Earth, the New Age in the Old Ways. And if you listen closely to the whispers in your soul, tuning in to the space where she dwells, you will see it has already begun. She lives, destroying the old and birthing the new within every soul, within every paradigm.

The rise of the Divine Feminine cannot be stopped. There are many people who feel threatened by her rising and will try to drag her back down, but to no avail. The Goddess is here—she lives on in you. She is the manifestation of your wildest dreams, the celebration of your freedom, and the joy of your satisfaction. Through your dedication to yourself and your love of All That Is, you are freeing the Goddess.

Your destined path with the Divine Feminine is ever-expanding, ever-evolving, never-ending. When you feel lost, reach out for her and let yourself be cradled. When you feel powerful, thank her for her blessings. When you feel loved, honor her by loving more. Wherever life leads you, whatever unfolds before you, trust the way forward. Always listen to the wisdom in your heart and let it lead you where you are meant to be led. There is no wrong way to walk with the Divine Feminine; there are no real mistakes. Everything you experience brings you lessons, gifts, and growth. Every moment provides you with the space to embrace your inner wise and wild woman. Every path always leads you back home to her, the goddess within.

STAY
CONNECTED

I am so honored that you have chosen to journey into your inner world and activate your inner goddess with me. I have grown so much myself throughout the writing of this book, and I hope that you feel the same after reading it. I am so proud of the woman I have become, and I am proud of you for choosing this path of self-devotion.

I would love to hear about your experiences while reading, and I would love to see any photos you take of your favorite entries.

If you post to Instagram, you can tag me @risingwithmorgan and use the hashtag #dailydfwisdom. On Twitter, you can tag me @risingwmorgan and use the same hashtag.

To learn more about how you can connect with me, visit my website: risingwithmorgan.com.

ABOUT
THE AUTHOR

Morgan Migliorisi is a witch, intuitive, and certified life coach. Over the last five years, she has worked with hundreds of women all over the world, helping them awaken their inner power and use it to craft lives they love. Morgan focuses on helping her clients understand themselves, discover their authentic voice, and find the courage to follow their heart's calling.

Morgan has built a loyal following on social media, where she shares daily motivational posts and holds conversations that inspire growth. She also offers a monthly membership through which you can connect with her daily for exclusive content and spiritual messages.

Website: risingwithmorgan.com

Hay House Titles of Related Interest

We hope you enjoyed this Hay House book. If you'd like to receive our online catalog featuring additional information on Hay House books and products, or if you'd like to find out more about the Hay Foundation, please contact:

Hay House, Inc., P.O. Box 5100, Carlsbad, CA 92018-5100
(760) 431-7695 or (800) 654-5126
(760) 431-6948 (fax) or (800) 650-5115 (fax)
www.hayhouse.com® • www.hayfoundation.org

———

Published in Australia by: Hay House Australia Pty. Ltd.,
18/36 Ralph St., Alexandria NSW 2015
Phone: 612-9669-4299 • *Fax:* 612-9669-4144
www.hayhouse.com.au

Published in the United Kingdom by: Hay House UK, Ltd.,
The Sixth Floor, Watson House, 54 Baker Street, London W1U 7BU
Phone: +44 (0)20 3927 7290 • *Fax:* +44 (0)20 3927 7291
www.hayhouse.co.uk

Published in India by: Hay House Publishers India,
Muskaan Complex, Plot No. 3, B-2, Vasant Kunj, New Delhi 110 070
Phone: 91-11-4176-1620 • *Fax:* 91-11-4176-1630
www.hayhouse.co.in

———

Access New Knowledge.
Anytime. Anywhere.

Learn and evolve at your own pace
with the world's leading experts.

www.hayhouseU.com

NOTES

NOTES

NOTES

NOTES

NOTES

NOTES